1798

Irish Reporter Publications: *Making History* Series
General Editors: Carol Coulter & Harry Vince

200 YEARS OF RESONANCE

ESSAYS AND CONTRIBUTIONS ON THE HISTORY AND RELEVANCE OF THE UNITED IRISHMEN AND THE 1798 REVOLUTION

Edited by Mary Cullen

IRISH
REPORTER
PUBLICATIONS

The editors wish to dedicate this book to
Sean Cudahy of New York,
1948-1997,
a constant supporter of
Irish Reporter Publications
from the beginning.

First published in 1998
by Irish Reporter Publications
c/o Nexus Ireland, Fumbally Court, Fumbally Lane, Dublin 8.

ISBN 1 - 900 900 - 03 - 3

Irish Reporter Series Number 28

Layout and Design: HVIS
Illustrations: Pages 13, 25, 26, 36, 67, 68, 73, 111, 112, 128, 143
courtesy of The National Museum of Ireland.
Cover photograph taken from the film
Bold Emmet Ireland's Martyr (1915)

Printed by Elo Press, Dublin

CONTENTS

Who Fears to Speak of Republicanism?
The Relevance of 1798

by Mary Cullen

> "In all social relations, it is our duty to preserve the interests of every individual, so as to make the good of each contribute to interests of the people. This is the true science of politics." (Jemmy Hope, United Irishman)

The relevance of 1798 for today must surely lie in how our perception of what happened then influences our understanding of how we have come to be where we are today and influences our perceptions of who we are.

We need then to try to understand the men and women of 1798 in their own time and on their own terms. This is not as easy as it may appear since the process of explaining what happened and why to suit vested interests had started even while it was in progress. However in recent years a new body of research has been growing which is deepening our knowledge of what did happen and why it happened, though it is important to remember that we by no means have the whole story yet. For example, the fact that women as well as men played an important role in the intellectual and political debate that gave birth to the United Irishmen is only beginning to be recognised.

Mary Cullen is an Academic Associate at the NUI, Maynooth, and a Research Associate at the Centre for Women's Studies, Trinity College, Dublin.

Some contributors are historians, who explain recent research and interpretations, others consider the significance of 1798 for later Irish history and today, from a variety of perspectives. We hope this edition will be a contribution both to an understanding of what happened and what we hope will be a vigorous debate about its relevance for today.

One major blind spot is that until recently there has been a tendency to undervalue the political thinking that drove the United Irishmen and their allies the Defenders. The core value of republican thinking in the 18th century was that government should both promote the good of the community as a whole and that the people as a whole should have a real say in that government. The words 'commonweal' and 'commonwealth' were widely used as English translations of the Latin *res publica*. Around that core value there was debate about the actual form of government and for some thinkers republicanism was even compatible with monarchy, if that monarchy could be seen to carry out the will of the people. Irish republicans, like republicans in other countries, could differ on how the people should have their say and on who should speak in their name.

The specific Irish political system which the United Irish societies aimed at first to reform and later to oust completely and replace was based on three major exclusions based on sex, class and religion. The first two exclusions were pretty universal at that period: holding public office, and, where elected representative bodies existed, sitting in them and voting at elections for them, were confined exclusively to a small property-owning minority of males. The third exclusion had its origins in the colonial relationship with England; the majority Catholic population was completely excluded from participation in political life, and the participation of Protestants who dissented from the Established Protestant Church was limited. Among these Protestant dissenters Presbyterians formed the largest group. The United Irish directly challenged the religious exclusion. It does not appear that many of them challenged the sex exclusion, though we know that the question was raised, notably by Mary Ann McCracken with her brother Henry. On the class exclusion, they believed that the interests of the people must be represented but did not necessarily all agree on how this should be done.

In the tradition of western republican thought some of the more radical thinkers had long argued that a redistribution of property was essential if the people as a whole were to have any real say. For example, in England as part of the 1640s' debates within Oliver Cromwell's New Model Army one group, the Levellers, argued for political republicanism, including universal manhood suffrage, while the Diggers went further and stressed the economic base needed for participation, including communal rights to the means of subsistence, essentially land, and individual rights to share in this. A decade later the English republican thinker James Harrington, in his book *Oceana* (1656), argued that in practice any political system came to reflect the actual distribution of property in a state. If all were to have a real input property must be widely and evenly distributed.

Recent research is showing that there was a strong social-radical content which linked social and economic inequality to political solutions in the thinking of some of the United Irish leaders, including among others Thomas Russell, Jemmy Hope and Henry Joy McCracken, and also in that of the Defenders, the vast underground organisation of the men and women of no property with whom the United Irishmen allied.

If the government of Ireland was to be reformed the United Irishmen believed from the first that it was essential to lessen English control over it. Separatism, establishing Ireland as an independent state separate from England, was not an integral part of Irish republican thinking at first, but came to be seen as such when Tone and the others became convinced that a republican form of government could not be achieved except by complete separation from England.

In 19th century Ireland there was considerable interaction between nationalism and republicanism. The belief that good government in Ireland could only be achieved when English control was lessened or removed underlay all nationalist movements in 19th century Ireland, including the Repeal movement of the 1840s and the later Home Rule movement. The beliefs that the removal of English control required complete separation and, if necessary, armed struggle to achieve it, and that social as well as political revolution was essential to achieve good government continued in the republican tradition. In the 1840s the Young Irelander James Fintan Lalor argued that a social revolution to nationalise the ownership of the land of Ireland was an essential part of the political revolution. In the 1850s the Fenians' proclamation of a provisional government included universal male suffrage and

3

declared that the soil of Ireland belonged to the people of Ireland. In the 1870s and 1880s Michael Davitt's vision of a New Departure in Irish politics was to join the aim of social revolution and the nationalisation of land with Home Rule. In the early 20th century James Connolly's primary objective was a socialist state, a workers' republic, and he believed that in Ireland a national revolution was an essential part of a socialist revolution. The 1916 Proclamation guaranteed equal rights and equal opportunities to all citizens and declared "its resolve to pursue the happiness and prosperity of the whole nation and all its parts, cherishing all children of the nation equally." (By this time Irish feminism was strong enough to ensure that the proclamation included women on equal terms with men.) In 1919 the Democratic Programme adopted by the First Dáil expressed similar objectives.

This is not to suggest that these ideas were always fully worked out and presented as coherent systems, or that they were always acted upon. For example, the Democratic Programme was clearly more honoured in the breach than the observance in the Irish Free State. The point is that the legacy of republican thinking persisted.

After partition and the setting up of the Northern Ireland state and the Irish Free State, the Republican movement did not recognise the legitimacy of the new structures and remained outside the public political process, aiming to reverse partition and put into effect the republic of 1916 and of the First and Second Dáils. It believed that a republic could only be achieved by complete separatism and in a 32-county Ireland, which should be achieved by physical force if necessary, and some Republicans believed in the need for social as well as political revolution. Internal differences as to the emphasis to be placed on either strand and the relationship between them led to tensions and splits, notably that in 1969-1970 from which emerged the Provisional IRA and Sinn Féin on the one hand and the Official IRA and Sinn Féin on the other. Today there is clearly difference of opinion within the IRA and Sinn Féin as to the possibility of achieving republican objectives by way of the current talks process and as to the wisdom of taking part in them.

The history of republicanism is central to the emergence of both the northern and southern states in Ireland today. If we can move the core value of republican thinking, that government should be in the interests of the people as a whole and that the people as a whole should have a major say in that government, to the centre of debate we may be able to open up new possibilities for real dialogue and progress. Many people who are not members of the Republican movement, who do not accept the use of armed struggle, who are undecided in their attitude to partition, do subscribe to the ideals of republican government.

One of the obstacles in the way of such a debate is the poverty of much of the media coverage and discussion of republicanism. Few media interviewers ask Republicans to explain their view of the kind of structures needed to create a truly republican society. There is in general a concentration on short-term confrontation and few commentators, in either the print or broadcast media, explore the underlying issues. A substantial amount of print comment consists largely of dismissive remarks rather than analysis. There is seldom any awareness of the historical context and a depressing tendency to accept the British establishment view that Irish Republicanism is a 'terrorism' that sprang spontaneously into life some thirty years ago.

If we are to develop a debate about republicanism today it must be in the context of the world of the late 1990s and not in that of 1798 or 1916 or 1921. In this world context we have seen the failure of the totalitarian communist regimes in eastern Europe to provide anything approaching the republican ideal of government and now we witness the similar failure of the global free-market economy and politics. We have learned that there are no easy blueprints sitting on the shelf waiting to be dusted off and put into practice. Nearer home a focus on what republicanism means would extend the debate beyond the narrow confines of an orange versus green dispute. Each of us carries a number of overlapping identities, and all of us on this island have been influenced and moulded by its history over the past 200 years. This is a many-faceted history in which none of us has lived in insulated solitude. For example, as a feminist I know how much I owe to the 19th century women's emancipationists, nearly all Protestant in religion and unionist in politics. They are part of my history and my identity as an Irish woman. Irish republicanism itself is an inclusive historical legacy that cuts across politico-religious divides. The United Irish organisation was based on the union of Protestant, Catholic and Dissenter - and indeed Presbyterian religious beliefs are seen as an important influence in developing Irish radical thinking in the 18th century.

The republican idea of government challenges today's Republican movement to address the question of how all the people, north and south, can have a say in their government. It also addresses this challenge to the rest of us. Many unionists and loyalists share a belief in the core values of historical republican thinking however much the baggage attached to the word in Ireland today may repel them. They need to be welcomed to the debate, invited to speak and, like everyone else, challenged as to how they would try to create structures in which all the people would have a say. In the south we live in a representative parliamentary democracy where everyone has the same right to vote and participate in the political process at all levels. How equal in fact is the possibility of real participation and how far does our system cherish all equally? We know that large numbers of people feel they have no effective say in politics and that their vote has little real meaning. Poverty, unemployment, sexual orientation can all be indicators of exclusion. Community activists demand their say in the development of their own areas, in identifying needs and devising solutions. Travellers challenge the organisation of society which accepts that their life expectancy, rates of illness, educational opportunities lag so far behind those of the settled community. Feminists argue that the politics of sex, the different political, social and economic consequences of biological sex, interact with all other discriminations. Recent events here in the south once more highlight the reality of the relationship between the distribution of wealth and political power.

A broad public debate about Irish republicanism would include many groups, many positions and many views. It would demand that they engage with each other, respect each other's right to speak, listen to each other's analysis and challenge each other in the search for an inclusive republican and democratic politics. Those of us who share the basic belief in republican government but who do not believe that today's circumstances justify the use of physical force to achieve it might consider whether we carry a responsibility to try to demonstrate that progress towards it is possible by other means. Deepening our understanding of 1798 could provide a base from which to launch the endeavour.●

The United Irishmen and the Revolution of 1798

An Outline View

by Tommy Graham

During the 1790s the United Irishmen attempted by various means to create an independent and democratic Irish republic. This process was to culminate in the revolution of 1798. Under the political system which existed at that time, which the United Irishmen sought originally to reform, and then eventually tried to overthrow in arms, only the 'Protestant Ascendancy', those professing the faith of the established Protestant church (Church of Ireland), only about ten per cent out of a population of five million, and who also possessed the necessary property qualifications, could participate fully in political life, either locally or nationally.

Tommy Graham is the joint Editor of *History Ireland* magazine and the secretary of the Dublin 1798 Commemoration Committee.

Over 90 per cent of the land was in the hands of Church of Ireland landowners of English origin, mostly acquired by conquest in the previous century, at the expense of Catholic landowners, both native Irish and 'Old' English. Although in theory independent, with the same monarch as Britain, the Kingdom of Ireland was controlled by the government in London, which restricted it both politically and economically. The vast majority were excluded from political life. These included Catholics, who made up the bulk of the peasantry, the middle classes of all denominations and the Presbyterians. The latter were largely descended from those Scots who settled in the north-eastern corner of Ireland in the previous century. Although usually better off than Catholics and better educated, Presbyterians were even more keenly aware of the disabilities they suffered. Consequently many of them emigrated to America during the course of the 18th century, in the hope of finding more tolerable political and economic conditions.

It is not surprising, therefore, that when the American colonists revolted against British government in the 1770s, they found a sympathetic ear amongst their kin in Ireland. In 1778, France - Britain's traditional enemy - entered the war on the American side, thus threatening Ireland with invasion. The British government was caught without an army to defend Ireland, since its regular troops had been sent to America and it did not have the revenue to raise an alternative, due to the economic dislocation caused by the war.

An Irish Protestant army, the Volunteers, was then raised to fill the breach, and financed locally. Unfortunately for the government it became the focus for various grievances, both political and economic and a convention of Ulster Volunteers (predominantly Presbyterian), at Dungannon in 1782, demanded parliamentary reform (a broadening of the franchise and the abolition of 'rotten' boroughs) and Catholic emancipation (the abolition of the remaining anti-Catholic laws). However a national Volunteer convention the following year split on the Catholic question and Volunteering declined thereafter.

The outbreak of the French Revolution in 1789, with its ideals of 'Liberty, Equality and Fraternity', provided fresh impetus to the reform movement in Ireland. In the autumn of 1791 Societies of United Irishmen were founded in Belfast and Dublin with the twin aims of parliamentary reform and Catholic emancipation.

The leading ideologue was Theobald Wolfe Tone, a Church of Ireland lawyer from Dublin, who, having witnessed the disarray of the Volunteers on the Catholic question some years earlier, was determined to forge a united reform movement of the various denominations. In addition he increasingly focused critical attention on the cornerstone of the existing Irish political system, which he identified as 'the connection with England', although his evolution into a fully fledged separatist and republican was to take a while longer. He found willing allies among the middle class leaders of the Catholic Committee who had recently displaced their more conservative landowning predecessors.

Determined to push more aggressively for concessions from government the new Catholic Committee appointed Tone as their secretary and over the course of 1792 mobilised for a 'Catholic Convention', held in the Tailors' Hall, in Dublin, that December. This Convention presented its demands directly to the London government, over the head of the implacably hostile Dublin administration. London, anxious to maintain the loyalty of the Catholic majority in the face of an impending war with revolutionary France, conceded almost all of the demands, except the right of Catholics to sit in parliament.

The Catholic Convention had a broad politicising effect, out of all proportion to the 233 delegates who directly participated. Delegates were elected in a series of meetings that reached down to parish level and involved broad sections of the people in political activity for the first time. The country was awash with a deluge of political pamphlets. In particular, the campaign politicised and broadened the horizons of the Defenders. This shadowy organisation first made its appearance in County Armagh, in the late 1780s, as a defence against the arms raids on Catholic premises by the 'Peep O'Day Boys', forerunners of the Orange Order, who were anxious to maintain the ban on Catholics bearing arms. By 1792-93 Defenderism had spread throughout south Ulster and north Leinster and it had even penetrated into Dublin City. Its propaganda had become more articulate and socially radical in tone. Throughout this period Tone, Samuel Neilson, Thomas Russell, and other radical United Irishmen, established contact with the Defenders, which was to provide the basis for a mass-based revolutionary United Irish organisation later in the decade.

Meanwhile the upholders of the *status quo* in Ireland were not idle in the face of these challenges. Along with the carrot of concessions to Catholics went the stick of repression: the Gunpowder Act which placed restrictions on firearms; the Militia Act, which envisaged a largely Catholic rank-and-file home defence force, officered by Protestants, and which provoked widespread disturbances; and the Convention Act, which outlawed any repeat of December 1792's 'Back Lane parliament'. The latter in particular stymied United Irish plans for a repeat of that success, on the issue of parliamentary reform.

An Ulster convention, dominated by United Irishmen demanding parliamentary reform met at Dungannon, in February 1793, just before the Convention Act was passed. The Dublin Society of United Irishmen was dispersed in May 1794, a fate shared by like-minded reform movements in England and Scotland. In the circumstances of Britain's war with revolutionary France demands for reform were equated with subversion. The war acted like a pressure-cooker, polarising the situation even further, and Ireland became a crucial theatre in this wider ideological struggle. At grassroots level the struggle was joined by the Defenders who became increasingly bold in their actions. As law-and-order deteriorated in the countryside government repression intensified, culminating in Commander-in-Chief Carhampton's brutal campaign against the Defenders in 1795.

Liberal Protestant opinion was outraged at the scale of the illegalities - many suspected Defenders were transported without a trial and the government responded with the Insurrection Act, which retroactively enshrined Carhampton's activities into law.

Sectarian hostilities flared up anew in County Armagh, culminating in the expulsion of thousands of Catholics and in the founding of the Orange Order, dedicated to the maintenance of Protestant ascendancy. With landlord and government sponsorship it spread rapidly over the following years, providing the government with a mass-based counter-revolutionary alternative to the United Irishmen. A more subtle variation within the overall counter-revolutionary strategy was the foundation of a Catholic seminary at Maynooth. Catholic seminarians would no longer be obliged to get educated in France, where many of them had developed an enthusiasm for the revolution. Thus the government cultivated the support of a Catholic hierarchy itself fearful of the spread of 'French principles'.

Earlier in 1795 the arrival of Fitzwilliam as Lord Lieutenant had raised Catholic hopes, only for them to be dashed by his sudden recall, having overstepped his brief. His successor, Camden, reinstated the policy of defending the Protestant Ascendancy at all costs. The United Irishmen, meanwhile, continued to meet clandestinely under various guises. The recall of Fitzwilliam removed whatever lingering hope they may have entertained for constitutional reform. The Catholic Committee dissolved itself (on the basis that "there was no longer a Catholic question only a national question"); a new constitution was drawn up for a single mass-based revolutionary United Irish organisation and Tone was dispatched to France (via America) in order to solicit military aid for an armed revolution.

By the end of 1796 Tone's mission had borne fruit, in the form of the dispatch of 16,000 French troops under General Hoche to Bantry Bay. Bad weather and bad seamanship, however, prevented the landing of this force, which in all probability could have liberated the country. Within Ireland, meanwhile, the United Irishmen had built up a formidable underground network, especially in Ulster where they claimed to have 100,000 armed and organised men. While they waited confidently for another French invasion attempt, government forces went on the offensive. Throughout the spring and summer of 1797 the army under General Lake, augmented by the Orange Order, was let loose on the people of Ulster. The 'dragooning of Ulster' effectively disarmed and crippled the United Irish organisation, especially in the middle and south of the province.

By the winter of 1797-98, with hopes of a renewed French attempt fading, the United Irishmen were forced to adopt a go-it-alone military strategy, focused on Dublin. Their organisation was strengthened in and around the capital and it also expanded in the south Leinster area. The planned insurrection was to have been a three-phased affair: the seizure of strategic positions within Dublin city, coordinated with the establishment of a crescent of positions outside, in north County Dublin, Meath, Kildare and Wicklow, and backed up by the engagement of government forces in the counties beyond to prevent reinforcement. Disaster struck on 12th March 1798, with the arrest of most of the Leinster leadership. Further arrests on the eve of the rising, in May, effectively decapitated the movement. The seizure of Dublin from within was aborted as they waited for orders that never came.

United Irish positions outside the city succumbed one by one; of the counties beyond, only in Wexford did the United Irishmen meet with success. A fortnight later (7th-9th June), despite the mauling at the hands of Lake's forces the year before, the United Irishmen of Antrim and Down managed to rise up, but they too were quickly defeated.

The Wexford insurgents met with a string of early successes but were ultimately prevented from spreading the insurrection beyond their own county by defeats at New Ross on the 5th June and at Arklow on the 9th June. Massive government forces began to move on Enniscorthy (21st June) for the decisive military showdown at Vinegar Hill.

Although the insurgents suffered defeats, the bulk of their forces escaped encirclement and carried on the struggle for another month, one group in the Wicklow mountains and the other in a 'long march' into the midlands, before being worn down and forced to surrender. A month later, on the 22nd August, over 1,000 French troops, under General Humbert, landed at Killala, County Mayo, but it was too little too late. Despite some initial successes, including a spectacular victory at Castlebar, Humbert and the United Irishmen who flocked to his standard were defeated at Ballinamuck, County Longford on the 8th of September. On the 17th of September a supply ship for Humbert, commanded by Napper Tandy, landed on Rutland Island in County Donegal, but withdrew on hearing news of Humbert's defeat. A month later another small French force, with Tone aboard, was intercepted by the British off Lough Swilly. The circumstances of Tone's death have been hotly disputed. While under sentence of death, following conviction for treason, he was discovered in his cell with a serious throat wound. In all probability it was self-inflicted. Tone wished to deny the authorities the satisfaction of a public hanging, rather than the military execution he thought was his due as an officer of the French Republic. He died of his wound on the 19th October. The insurrection of 1798 was over.

The United Irishmen suffered defeat in 1798, but their immediate adversary, the Protestant Ascendancy, also lost position. Two years later the Act of Union abolished its Parliament in College Green and Ireland was ruled directly from London. Some United Irishmen (especially Presbyterians) welcomed the abolition of this corrupt assembly as a form of parliamentary reform.

Many Catholics (especially the hierarchy and gentry) welcomed it as a harbinger of their admission to full political rights. They were to be disappointed: Catholic Emancipation only came a generation later, in 1829. By that stage the context had changed: what had become a national question reverted to being purely a Catholic one.

The emergence of the politics of the headcount, of confessional 'majorities' and 'minorities', increasingly displaced and obscured the mass-democratic, non-sectarian ideals of the United Irishmen, based on principles such as the rights of man and the rights of nations, ideals which still have a relevance in the Ireland of today ●

Battle of New Ross, June 5th, 1798

Irish Film Archive Screenings

Institute of Ireland

- 27th and 28th February
  1798 on Film
  A screening of all known documentary and fiction material relating to the 1798 Rebellion.

- 18th and 19th March
  Two films by Prof. George C Stoney, New York University
  Prof. Stoney will present two of his documentary films, *How the Myth was Made* (1978) and *The Uprising of '34* (1996).

- 16th April
  The Rocky Road to Dublin (1968)
  This controversial documentary about Dublin will be introduced by its director, Peter Lennon.

- 28th May
  Men for the Harvest (1963)
  This RTE documentary about Maynooth seminary has not been seen since its first transmission in 1963.

The Irish Film Archive preserves and makes permanently accessible Ireland's film heritage. If you are aware of any film or film related materials the Irish Film Archive would be interested in hearing from you.

6, Eustace Street, Temple Bar, Dublin 2, Ireland. Telephone (353 1) 679 5744; Fax 677 8755; e-mail ifc@iol.ie and web site http://www.iftn.ie/ifc

The Defenders

The Other Great Movement of the Late Eighteenth Century

by Deirdre Lindsay

"Defenderism puzzles me more and more" wrote Edward Cooke, Dublin Castle's intelligence expert, in September 1795. A shrewd and well-informed official, Cooke was not often given to expressions of puzzlement, but his uncertainty on this subject has been echoed over the years by historians of the 1790s, who, rather like the officials of the Irish government at the time, have tried to put to put together an accurate picture of the nature and extent of revolutionary activity in Ireland in that decade.

Deirdre Lindsay is a teacher of history at St Mary's College, Derry.
She is researching Irish politics in the 1790s and lives in County Tyrone

That picture is of course dominated by the United Irishmen who led the outbursts of open rebellion in 1798. But as all major studies of the period show, the story of the United Irishmen's insurrection cannot properly be understood without reference to their fellow conspirators, the Defenders. This being so, it is remarkable that this group has not yet been the focus for a comprehensive study in its own right. Nevertheless, while a definitive history of the Defenders remains to be written, the wealth of research and writing generated by the 1790s has provided insights into the nature of Defender activity, the importance of the Defenders and their relevance to the insurrection of 1798.

Who were the Defenders? Traditional accounts have viewed them as simply another manifestation of the oath-bound, agrarian secret society which was a perennial feature of the Irish countryside from the mid-eighteenth century onwards. There is evidence that some contemporaries considered them in this light: Thomas Conolly referred in 1793 to "Oakboys, Steelboys, Whiteboys, Rightboys, Peep of Day Boys and Defenders - all of which I have seen in my time". The 19th century historian, Lecky, referred to the Defenders as "a new Whiteboy movement", and, writing some 90 years later, McDowell placed the Defenders in the category of "rural rioters", acting primarily on economic grievances which, in County Armagh, were "interfused with religious animosity". Recent research, however, reveals the Defenders to have been a more complex organisation which defies easy classification.

The origins of the Defender movement have been well documented and the main elements of the story are not disputed. Defenders first appeared in north Armagh, in the Markethill area, during a series of localised conflicts, or faction fights, among peasants. The conflict seems to have arisen over a trivial personal dispute and the opposing sides (the Nappach Fleet and Hamiltons Bawn Fleet- names reflecting local townlands) initially comprised both Catholics and Protestants. From 1785 however the conflict took on a sectarian aspect: the Nappach Fleet began to attack the homes of Catholics in the area to capture their weapons and the victims began to organise themselves into defence associations. Subsequently the opposing sides became realigned into Protestant Peep O'Day Boys (so-called because of their dawn raids on Catholic homes) and Catholic Defenders (although the Defenders of Bunkershill in Armagh initially had a Presbyterian

16

'captain'). The 'Armagh disturbances' which recurred over the next few years have been described by Nancy Curtin as

> full scale sectarian warfare characterised by ritualised acts of intimidatory intrusion into disputed territory and nightly raids to disarm opponents.

However if one is to explain why the Defender movement spread beyond the immediate vicinity of this dispute one must look at the long term causes of the trouble.

Why did such serious sectarian conflict occur in this area? Many explanations have emphasised the importance of economic rivalry between peasants in an area where the population was equally divided between Anglican, Presbyterian and Catholic: some writers have argued that the competition for land intensified after the Catholic Relief Acts of 1778 and 1782, which allowed Catholics to compete for land on a more equal footing; others have stressed the importance of developments in the linen trade, particularly the general discontent arising from the decline of small-scale independent weaving and the growing dependence of weavers on outside entrepreneurs (bleachers and putters-out).

To these primarily economic explanations have been added factors such as the relatively recent losses of land among high-ranking Gaelic families and a corresponding deeply-felt sense of loss of status among key families locally. In all these explanations the agrarian background of the Defenders is stressed. While all of these factors may, as Marianne Elliott has suggested be "the local conditions conducive to the development of Defenderism" in Armagh they do not explain the spread of the Defender movement into other areas, where the economic structures differed considerably, nor do they account for the development of the Defenders into what Nancy Curtin has called "potentially the nation's most revolutionary body".

The factor which seems to account for the development of Defenderism and also to distinguish the Defenders from similar agrarian movements is the issue of political rights for Catholics. In the 1780s this issue revolved around the right of Catholics to bear arms. 'Catholic relief' (i.e., the removal of legal disabilities which Catholics were subject to since the Glorious Revolution) was a source of political debate from the 1750s onwards and the question of the right of Catholics to bear arms was aired regularly, particularly as the question was crucial to the admission of Catholics to the British armed forces, as well as having a bearing on civilian rights. In the early 1780s the question was highlighted by the debate over whether Catholics should be admitted into the civilian Volunteer Corps.

The importance of political factors in the origin and subsequent development of the Defenders is argued particularly by Louis Cullen, who claims that political circumstances in County Armagh played a crucial part in the Armagh disturbances in the mid-1780s and their revival in the early 1790s. In essence Cullen argues that the troubles developed from the arming during this local dispute of some Catholics with the full support of a radical section of Protestant political opinion in the county. The arming of Catholics became a divisive issue in Armagh because it represented the granting of political rights to Catholics. This fundamentally political ingredient is the only factor which can adequately explain the spread of Defenderism into the neighbouring counties of Louth and Meath, and into areas of north Connaught, particularly Sligo and Roscommon. These areas shared with County Armagh a hardline Protestant political establishment at county level, men who took a tough stance in support of the penal laws and against the admission of Catholics into the Volunteers.

Cullen's interpretation of Defender origins relies on a close scrutiny of political factors at county and local level. However his broad thesis that Defender organisations "grew out of unrest which was political rather than agrarian or industrial" is supported by other research. Elliott has noted that the worst Defender disturbances occurred in areas where the leading gentry were noted "anti-papists", and that although Defenders were usually Catholic, they were not always motivated by anti-Protestantism. Instead they voiced resentment over "blanket Protestant control of society", particularly their dominance of local life and the system of justice. Where justice was thought to be administered impartially, Defenderism was weak. Neither were the Defenders particularly anti-landlord: their attacks on the Hill family in County Down were unusual and seem to have stemmed from that family's high-profile stance against 'Popery'.

Elliott draws a distinction between the Defenders and the agrarian bands in the Whiteboy tradition, which continued to operate sporadically during these years and whose aims and methods remained wholly traditional. The social aims of the Defenders were fairly traditional (e.g., the desire to regulate the payment of tithes, church cess, dues paid to the priests and rents - particularly rents for potato ground) and for many Defenders, perhaps, the realisation of these aims would have sufficed. The Defenders certainly tended to adapt their programme to incorporate local grievances in the areas in which they operated, but from the early 1790s their demands were revolutionary in tone: "We have lived long enough upon potatoes and salt; it is our turn now to eat mutton and beef".

There were also inherent differences in method, organisation, social composition and wider political aims which distinguished the Defenders from agrarian groups. The Defenders, it is claimed, did not generally attack and destroy property or livestock but primarily conducted raids on private houses (often of Protestants) for arms. They also met by night in large numbers, to practise military drill and to swear-in new members. There is some disagreement among historians over the extent to which they were involved in committing 'outrages' (violent attacks on property or persons). The tendency among the authorities to label every form of disturbance as 'Defenderism' has no doubt made the issue of the nature of Defenders' actions more difficult to assess.

The Defenders displayed a more sophisticated organisational structure with a greater degree of coordination between different areas than previously seen in the localised agrarian groups. This is evident from contemporary reports of "the appearance of method" in their plans; the standardised oaths and the system of signs and secret passwords which operated. The extent to which this applied throughout different parts of the country can be overstated: the Defenders did not form a single coherent organisation. Nevertheless the existence of a system of coordination is significant. The influence of Freemasonry is evident in some aspects of the organisation as well as in the adoption of the term 'lodge' and in the system of numbering Defender lodges (for which there is evidence as early as 1789 in County Louth).

On the question of the social composition of the Defenders it would be incorrect to consider them a peasant movement. Elliott in particular argues strongly that their strength lay in the urban and industrialised areas and among the same social element in rural areas: "The Defenders were only one step nearer the peasantry than the United Irishmen." Defenders were drawn from among weavers, labourers and tenant farmers who were also involved in some kind of domestic industry and from the growing artisan class in the towns. Geographically the Defenders were strongest in Ulster, north Connaught and north Leinster. Kevin Whelan asserts that they "never penetrated into the old heartlands of the secret societies in east Munster and south Leinster". The strength of the Defenders in urban environments, particularly Dublin, belies any notion that they were a peasant or Whiteboy-type movement. In addition, whereas elsewhere the Defenders tended to be exclusively Catholic, it is interesting to note that in Dublin there were Protestant Defenders.

By 1795 there were reportedly some 4,000 Defenders in and around Dublin. Undoubtedly, as Smyth has found, the spread of Defenders in Dublin was facilitated by the pre-existence of illegal 'combinations' (proto-trade unions) among the journeymen manufacturers in the city:

> Journeymen combinations served as a model for the urban Defender lodges and many Dublin Defenders were already, through their experience of combinations, well versed in the techniques and ethos of the secret society.

As well as nascent trade union organisations, Dublin by the early 1790s had political clubs and reading societies based on the city's journeymen and artisans - the Telegraphic and Philanthropic Societies and other 'Jacobin clubs' such as 'the Originals' and 'the Sons of Freedom'. Dublin's politicised lower class was therefore fertile ground for Defenderism.

Defenderism was also imported into Dublin by means of the migration of rural workers to the city. Two of the Defenders tried for high treason in Dublin in 1795 - Weldon and Hart - were originally Meathmen and further evidence exists of the links between Dublin Defenders and Meath. Additional ways in which Defenderism spread to Dublin are evident in the observation by a Dublin Defender that:

> I never heard of any (Defenders) being in Dublin until the militiamen came and I am sure it was them and the Defenders that ran away from the country that first brought it to Dublin.

This points to the likelihood that rural Defenders, fleeing prosecution to the relative anonymity of the city, accounted for the initial spread of Defenderism in Dublin. Secondly, the role of militiamen in spreading the Defender system is highlighted.

When, in 1793, the government set up a Militia - a new civilian peacekeeping force, controversially including Catholics, the system which they used to levy the new force was local 'balloting'. This enforced recruitment led to sworn Defenders being compelled into new County regiments, which were then posted to other parts of the country. The government therefore contributed to the spread of "the contagion of Defenderism" to previously unaffected parts of the country. Defender penetration of the Militia and similar attempts by the United Irishmen to recruit these soldiers posed a significant threat to the government. The response was effective: the execution early in 1797 of four Monaghan militiamen caught spreading United Irish ideas at Blaris Camp near Belfast, described by Thomas Bartlett as a "carefully managed exercise in official terror", has been seen as a turning point for the authorities in stemming the spread of revolutionary ideas among a key social group, the military.

To understand the development of the Defenders one must look not only at the immediate political and social context out of which they emerged but also at the wider political picture. The impact of the national agitation for Catholic Relief between 1791 and 1793 has been highlighted by several historians as awakening a political consciousness among people previously excluded from politics. A blaze of publicity surrounded the issue of the admission of Catholics to the political nation and the country-wide campaign undertaken by the Dublin-based Catholic Committee linked the question with immediate social and economic gains for the wider Catholic population, raising political expectations, often to unrealistic levels. The intense political activity throughout Ireland during 1792, with elections held at parish and county level for delegates to the Catholic Convention of December, opened up political participation to Catholics, stimulated the political agenda of the Defenders and lent a certain 'millenarian zest' to some Defender activities. As Whelan has commented: "Defenderism represented the democratisation of the political culture of Catholics, and a definitive break with the century-old strategy of supplication".

Conversely, this assertive Catholic campaign served to heighten the anxieties and fears of Protestant Ascendancy interests who, although forced under British government pressure to concede the parliamentary franchise to propertied Catholics, nevertheless gave vent to their hostility and resentment in anti-Catholic tirades in parliament and in increasing repression of Defender activity in the country.

Popular politicisation was without doubt a result of the Catholic Committee's reform campaign of 1793, but the wider political context should not be overlooked: namely, the seismic impact of the French revolution on Ireland. This is usually viewed in terms of its effects on the 'political nation' (i.e., men of property) but its effect on popular political protest can also be detected in the language used by the Defenders. In contrast with the local and obtainable aims of previous secret societies, the Defenders spoke of revolutionary change. In their oaths, catechisms, and handbills, they spoke of "overturning the King's government in this Kingdom." They swore to

> quell all nations, to dethrone all kings and plant the Tree of Liberty in our Irish land whilst the French Defenders will protect our cause, and the Irish Defenders pull down British laws.

In Defender oaths, however, the planting of the 'Tree of Liberty' was sometimes replaced by planting of the 'True Religion'. This idea of overturning the Protestant church establishment and reversing the plantation land settlement was a common motif: "they can never forget that they have been the proprietors of this country". Revenge against Protestants was certainly an important element in Defender thinking and one which, juxtaposed as it sometimes was with the expectation of assistance from revolutionary France, indicates the unsophisticated nature of the Defenders' political thinking. Given the political context out of which the Defenders emerged, the politicising impact of the Catholic relief campaign and the influence of new ideas from France, it is perhaps not surprising that Defender aims often mixed old Catholic grievances over dispossession and religious persecution with new Republican ideas. Whelan has examined this further, contrasting the Enlightenment ideas of the United Irishmen with the 'cultural nationalism' of the Defenders:

particularists not universalists, exclusive not inclusive, realists not Utopians, Defenderism articulated a different world view to that of the United Irishmen.

This brings us to the question of the part played by the Defenders in the conspiracy which led to the 1798 insurrection. Most historians agree that contacts between the Defenders and the United Irishmen date from at least 1794-95 and that a formal alliance had been forged by early 1797. Cullen has claimed that links between the Defenders and the United Irishmen date from earlier than 1794 pointing to the United Irish missions throughout Ulster during 1792 and 1793 as evidence not only of efforts at recruitment, but the opening up of negotiations with Defenders. This development was exactly what the government was striving to prevent throughout the 1790s: a link up between the widespread network of Defender clubs with their volatile methods and vaguely defined political aspirations, and the smaller scale United Irish organisation with its largely middle class leadership, radical Presbyterian grassroots, French military allies and overtly revolutionary objectives.

To writers who stress the economic grievances of the Defenders, and the sectarian nature of their activities, such an alliance has been seen as 'unnatural'. However, if one accepts the political nature of Defenderism, the reasons for the conjunction become clearer. Both organisations shared a deepening hostility to Ascendancy interests and their anti-reform policies. They also shared a commitment to the ideas of revolutionary France and a readiness to seek assistance from the French. They differed, of course, in many ways, most importantly perhaps in their vision of what was to replace the 'junto' in Ireland.

The advantages of the alliance for the United Irishmen are obvious: the existing Defender lodges provided a ready-made network of allies in the forthcoming armed confrontation with government forces. In addition they offered avenues into new recruiting grounds, both in geographical and social terms, for the United Irish system. For the Defenders the contacts with the United Irish Society were consolidated through the active support given by the United Irishmen during the government's increasing repression of Defender activity from 1795 onwards. Thomas Graham has noted that at this time Dublin Castle saw the greatest threat coming from the Defenders, and the government responded with a series of legislative, judicial and military measures aimed primarily at halting the spread of 'disaffection'. Draconian action was taken by Lord Carhampton in north Connaught, when he arrested and sent to the fleet over one thousand suspects, an illegal action for which the government later made allowance with a retrospective Indemnity Act. The prosecution and execution of Defenders intensified in Armagh, Dublin and elsewhere and an extraordinary piece of emergency-powers legislation was enacted (the 1796 Insurrection Act). These developments, along with the growing loyalist political reaction represented by the development and spread of the Orange Order, left the Defenders increasingly at the mercy of reactionary authorities. The provision of professional legal expertise, financial, and other practical assistance by the United Irishmen in this period, while demonstrating the 'brotherhood of affection' which was a founding principle of the United Irishmen, was also part of a deliberate strategy to build 'an union of power' among Irishmen, specifically, in this case, with the Defenders.

The fruits of this Defender-United Irish alliance can be seen in the increasing numbers of Defenders who were joining United Irish cells, particularly in Dublin, Kildare and Meath, from 1796 onwards. These Defender recruits remained, according to Graham, "comparatively well-organised and disciplined in the United system" throughout 1797 and 1798. In parts of Ulster, it seems, individual Defender recruitment into the United Irishmen did not generally occur, but rather Defender cells were brought within the United Irish command structure.

The advanced nature of Defender organisation may have been one reason for this, but, ironically, it was probably more due to the practical difficulties faced by the United Irishmen in overcoming sectarian tensions in some areas. This strategy is seen as contributing to the failure of Ulster United Irishmen to rise, outside Counties Antrim and Down, in 1798. The branch structure of the Defenders, remaining as it did independent of the United Irish chain of command, rested primarily on a few individuals. Similarly, the links between the two organisations depended on a handful of key figures (such as Samuel Neilson, Thomas Russell, Henry Joy McCracken of the United Irishmen and the Teeling family, James Quigley and John Magennis of the Defenders) - a "common alliance of leaders on both sides" - who had worked closely together for a number of years.

The government's success in 1798 turned on the arrests of key leaders in Ulster and Leinster, which not only threw the United Irish plans into some doubt, but effectively cut the links of personal trust and cooperation upon which the conspiratorial alliance depended. The effectiveness of government repression, particularly in Ulster in 1797, greatly weakened the conspiracy, and the 1798 arrests jeopardised the active strategy of coordinated action by the Defenders and United Irishmen.

However the factor which finally neutralised the threat of united military action by Defenders and United Irishmen was the revival of sectarian fears, both by the design of interested parties throughout the period, and by accident, as events unfolded during the summer of 1798. Historians are only just beginning to understand the complexity of the ebb and flow of loyalty and disloyalty, revolution and reaction, in Ireland in this period. The Defender movement, "the other great movement of the late eighteenth century", played a central role in Irish society in the 1790s as a potent political force and our increasing understanding of that role is beginning to inform our understanding of what happened in 1798.

Suggested further reading:
N Curtin, *The United Irishmen*, Oxford, 1994;
D Dickson, D Keogh, and K Whelan (eds), *The United Irishmen*,
Dublin, 1993 (Chapters by LM Cullen, M Elliott, T Graham,
and K Whelan);
M Elliott, *Partners in revolution: the United Irishmen and France*,
Yale, 1982.
H Gough and D Dickson (eds), *Ireland and the French Revolution*,
Dublin, 1990 (Chapters by J Smyth and LM Cullen);
G O'Brien, *Parliament, Politics and People*,
Dublin,1989 (Chapter by J Smyth) ●

Henry Joy McCracken

Surrender of General Humbert at Ballinamuck, September 8th, 1798

The Men of No Popery
The Origins of the Orange Order

by Jim Smyth

We'll fight to the last in the honest old cause,
And guard our religion, our freedom and laws,
We'll fight for our country, or king and our crown,
And make all the traitors and croppies lie down.

Jim Smyth lectures in history at the University of Notre Dame, Indiana. His work includes the book *The Men of No Property*. This article is linked to one published in *History Ireland*.

As well as stimulating radical revivals right across Europe the French Revolution polarised politics everywhere. In each country the revivified radical movements confronted conservative and royalist crusades against 'Jacobinism', the name derived from the radical democratic politics of the Jacobin clubs in France. Sir Richard Musgrave, the loyalist historian of the rebellion, and himself an Orangeman, made the point:

> In the year 1792 when the dissemination of treason and the formation of seditious clubs in London threatened the immediate destruction of the constitution ... loyal societies checked the progress and baneful effects of their doctrines. The institution of the Orangemen did not differ from them in the smallest degree.

The Orange Order was forged in the crucible of sectarian conflict in County Armagh. The formation of Orange Lodge No. 1 followed a violent clash between armed Protestant bands and Defenders at a crossroads hamlet, named the Diamond, near the village of Loughgall. Up to 30 Defenders were killed that 'running Monday', the 21st of September 1795, while none of the surviving accounts records any fatalities on the Protestant side. The 'Battle of the Diamond' ranks as one of the more bloody encounters in a sequence of disturbances between the Protestant Peep O'Day Boys and the Defenders, stretching back to the mid 1780s. The Defenders, as the name indicates, began as Catholic bands formed to defend themselves against the Peep O'Day Boys. The origins of this conflict which gave rise to the Orange Order has to be sought in the interaction of social, economic and political factors.

Armagh, the most densely populated county in the country, was a microcosm of late 18th century Ireland. Each of the three major religious denominations was represented there, in roughly equal proportions: a Catholic majority in the poorer south; an Episcopalian (Church of Ireland) majority in the north; and Presbyterians most numerous across the centre. Each confessional group had a corresponding ethnic identity, Irish-Catholic, Scots-Presbyterian and English-Episcopalian, and each was present to some degree in all areas of the county. That finely balanced religious demography itself helps to account for the persistent sectarian tensions. Patterns of settlement, dating back to the 17th century plantation, created 'cultural frontiers', flash points of territorial dispute and inter-communal strife. Because of their numbers Catholics appeared more threatening to their Protestant neighbours than in counties such as Antrim and Down where they were a clear minority. The Presbyterian farmers of Antrim and Down, who later embraced the union of Protestant, Catholic and Dissenter in the United Irishmen, felt safe to do so. In Armagh it was different. When the masonic lodges of Antrim, Down, Derry and Tyrone supported parliamentary reform, in the winter of 1792-3, the Armagh masons condemned them. Reform - or innovation as they denounced it - brought the simultaneous campaign for Catholic relief too close for comfort.

An explosive religious geography reacted upon an unstable social structure and local economy. That endemic unrest used to be explained by land hunger. Following the repeal in 1778 and 1782 of penal laws restricting Catholic access to landed property, Catholic competition for leases intensified, driving up prices and provoking Protestant resentment. Then in 1793 the Catholic Relief Act gave the parliamentary vote to 'forty-shilling freeholders' in the counties, thus increasing the political value of Catholic tenants to landlords.

More recent explanations of the Armagh troubles stress the destabilising effects of modernisation (including the spread of a money-based economy) and the political dimensions of the Peep O'Day backlash; but many witnesses at the time linked land competition to sectarian rivalry. Rather than simply discounting the land issue as the cause of the disturbances, it needs to be integrated with newer theories as one cause among several.

In fact the economic importance of land was diminishing during this period. Late 18th century Armagh experienced rapid social change, generated by its thriving linen industry. Much of the linen-led commercial and manufacturing expansion of the Irish economy at this time centred on Ulster's 'linen triangle', an area comprising west County Down, north Armagh and mid Tyrone. Linen, produced for sale in the market place by piece-working and wage-earning journeymen weavers, transformed rural society. By the 1790s in some parts of the county agriculture was supplementing income from spinning, weaving and bleaching rather than the reverse.

Armagh, noted a contemporary observer, "is a hotbed of cash". Inevitably the scale and pace of modernisation loosened the deference-based social controls on which the 'natural leadership' of the gentry had traditionally rested. Apprentices and young journeymen who 'got the handling of cash' before they knew the value of it, enjoyed an independence of action absent from the forelock-tugging dependency culture of landed society.

Whereas Catholic competition in the land market allegedly drove up the price of leases, Catholic weavers competing in the labour market aroused Protestant hostility by allegedly depressing wage rates. Certainly, substantial Catholic participation in the linen boom is not in doubt. Prominent Catholic radicals such as Luke Teeling in Lisburn and Bernard Coile in Lurgan, were wealthy linen merchants. A brother of James Coigly, the Armagh priest, Defender and United Irishman, employed up to 100 'hands' in the county. From the standpoint of Protestant ascendancy the Catholic menace included a threat to the livelihoods of Protestant weavers. During the 1780s, Peep O'Day Boys raiding Catholic homes (which were also their workplaces) in search of arms, smashed domestic looms whenever they came across them. Again, the wholesale 'wrecking' of Catholic cottages by Orangemen in the winter of 1795-6 included the destruction of looms, webs and yarn. The breakdown of traditional social control lurched into sectarian economic warfare.

Rapid economic change, population pressure and religious geography combined to produce a particularly volatile situation in late 18th century Armagh. The disturbances, however, had a political detonator: under the Penal Laws Catholics were denied the right to bear arms - a proscription which had symbolic and political as well as practical significance. In an age of citizens' militias and deep distrust of standing armies, the right of the people to bear arms guaranteed their liberty and property. That at least was the theory.

The Irish Volunteers, formed in Ulster in 1778, embodied classical republican and Whig ideas of armed citizenship, public virtue and legitimate resistance to tyranny. A few years later the right to bear arms was ratified in the written constitution of the new American republic.

Thus, in the mid 1780s when certain Volunteer companies in Ulster, Dublin and elsewhere admitted Catholics to their ranks, they unilaterally, and illegally, admitted them to fuller citizenship. According to another report, at about the same time the Armagh *grandee* Lord Gosford armed local Catholics for the less exalted purpose of protecting his orchards from pilfering!

Arms raids were political. The disarming of Catholics in County Armagh amounted to a spontaneous and unilateral attempt by lower-class Protestants to reaffirm Protestant ascendancy by re-enforcing the Penal Laws. The Defenders, as already noted, emerged as Catholic bands, formed to defend themselves against the Peep O'Day Boys. But, as the Defenders became pro-active and politicised and spread into south Ulster and the midlands their standard tactic of raiding the houses of gentry for firearms echoed the original Peep O'Day Boy campaign, and in the context of the Penal Laws that tactic was charged with political symbolism. In part arms raids represented an assertion by lower-class Catholics of equal status under the law.

At a local level the Peep O'Day Boys tried to maintain a system of privilege built upon religious discrimination. Yet in the 18th century popular anti-Catholicism could assume many different forms. Although it fed on the sort of vulgar prejudices concerning superstition and priestcraft so deftly parodied in the writings of Wolfe Tone, and although it could degenerate into the kind of hysterical bigotry personified by Sir Richard Musgrave, it had a positive side. To republicans and Whigs, from John Milton in the 1650s to William Drennan, Volunteer and future United Irishman, in the 1780s, Catholics were justly excluded from the constitution on the grounds that tolerance could not safely be extended to the intolerant, nor liberty to its enemies. Those antipathies, historically rooted in Whig myths of the 'Glorious Revolution' of 1688 in England and Irish Protestant folk memories of the 1641 rebellion and of their deliverance from popish tyranny by William of Orange at the Boyne in 1690, were sustained by contemporary perceptions of the despotic monarchy of France. Catholics, wrote Drennan, were "unfit for liberty". Alongside its popular pedigree, the Orange Order, the successor to the Peep O'Day Boys, who celebrated the 'religion, freedom and laws', also had a radical and subversive potential which troubled the men of property and the government from the start.

Orange and United Irish societies shared a common ancestry in both Volunteering and Freemasonry. As a form of participation in public life the Volunteering experience raised levels of political awareness, but it did not predetermine the content of politicisation. While some of the Volunteer companies recruited Catholics, others remained aggressively protestant. The Volunteers who clashed with Defenders in Armagh in 1788, or at Rathfriland, County Down, in 1792, were denounced as little more than Peep O'Day Boys in uniform. The societies of United Irishmen, established at Belfast and Dublin in 1791, were composed of veteran Volunteers; so, too, were the first Orange lodges. The decisive Protestant victory at the battle of the Diamond has been attributed to superior firepower, occupation of the high ground, and 'old Volunteer discipline'.

Freemasonry in 18th century Europe had developed a widespread network of lodges, which were not confined to stonemasons, but open to men of all religions, social classes and political views. The lodges served as clubs, often meeting in taverns, for social enjoyment and mutual assistance. Irish Freemasonry was expanding rapidly during the heyday of Volunteering, particularly in the Volunteer heartlands of Ulster and Dublin. Indeed in several cases Masonic lodges and Volunteer companies merged. Lodges and companies, with their regalia and uniforms, answered largely the same social and recreational demands, and the number of associations in the north testifies to the density and richness of popular culture in Ulster. By 1804 there were 43 recognised or 'warranted' Masonic lodges in Armagh, 92 in neighbouring Tyrone and 56 in County Down.

Masonic secrecy applied only to the internal ritual and business of craft, not to membership. For example, in October 1784 a Masonic funeral held at Loughgall - the site of the original Defender-Peep O'Day Boy feud - included 1,000 Volunteers and '300 Masons in regular procession'. It is no surprise that such a common style of association provided others, sometimes Masons themselves, with a ready-made model. The fledgling Orange Order (and the Defenders and United Irishmen) borrowed wholesale from Masonic practice and terminology. The Orange 'lodges', 'masters', 'grand masters', 'oaths', 'signs', 'degrees', 'warrants' and 'brethren' all have a clear Masonic lineage. Sketching in the background to the Battle of the Diamond, Musgrave alleged that

> in the year 1795, the Romanists, who assumed the name of masons, used frequently to assemble in the neighbourhood of Loughgall, Charlemont, Richhill, Portadown, Lurgan ... and robbed the Protestants of their arms.

On the 18th of September, three days before the battle, a local gentleman informed the Dublin government that "the Protestants who call themselves Freemasons go in lodges and armed", while 40 years later a witness before a parliamentary inquiry recalled that the first Orangemen had employed secrecy

> to afford protection, if they could, to those who refused to join the United Irishmen; for every act of intimidation was used, and the fondness of the people for associating together, their attachment to Freemasonry, and all those private associations, gave a particular zest to this mode of keeping them to their allegiance.

James Wilson and James Sloan, who along with 'Diamond' Dan Winter, issued the first Orange lodge warrants from Sloan's Loughgall inn, were masons.

The "fondness of the people for associating together", for joining, oath-taking and 'secret' collecting, also helps to explain the apparently baffling phenomenon of Orange and Masonic lodges defecting to the United Irishmen and vice versa. These crossovers, which can be accounted for at one level by local political pressures, intimidation and bandwagoning were, at the very least, facilitated by the popular 'fondness' for joining, belonging and secrecy.

Despite their militant loyalism and anti-revolutionary ideology, there were remarkable parallels between the early Orange lodges and the Defender-United Irish alliance that had emerged by 1795. Both were popular movements; both had antecedents in Freemasonry and Volunteering; and both thrived in the divided, densely textured, modernising society and economy of Ulster.

The first of these similarities concerned the government and its supporters most. Dan Winter was a publican and the first lodge masters included tailors, 'linen inspectors' and inn keepers. One early lodge, no. 7, met in a disused lime kiln. Other lodges, echoing 'hedge' or 'unwarranted' masonry, were known as 'hedgers' or 'ditchers' from their practice of assembling "behind hedges and in dry ditches".

Later apologists rather implausibly deny any connection between the Peep O'Day Boys and the first Orangemen or, even less plausibly, between the Orangemen and the mass 'wrecking' of Catholic cottages in Armagh in the months following the Diamond; all of them, however, acknowledge the movement's lower class origins. As one sympathetic, but socially 'respectable' chronicler of these years put it, Protestant farmers and linen manufacturers, all

> humble men ... decided to have a system of their own creation, and to control it themselves ... an organisation formed and fashioned by their own hands, and outside the control of landed proprietors, agents, bailiffs, baronial constables, and all the rest.

Predictably, that robust spirit of independence in turn excited the "decided antagonism of some of the gentry". Local gentry families, such as the Blackers and the Verners, were involved in the Orange Order within weeks of its formation and the men of property effected a virtual takeover within about 18 months, a process culminating in the establishment of a Grand National Lodge boasting several peers and prominent Protestant ultras, in Dublin in 1798. In spite of this Orangeism began as a popular initiative. The gentry assumed leadership as a means of reasserting control over a volatile tenantry. Generals Lake and Knox grudgingly harnessed the Orangemen as a counter-insurgency force during a period of crisis, but many magistrates remained distrustful. From the outset Orangeism had a respectability problem.

The county élites and the government moved quickly to co-opt a movement, denounced by Lord Gosford as a "lawless banditti", because it proliferated at such an astonishing rate. Some 2,000 Orangemen marched on the first 12th of July commemoration, at Lurgan-Portadown in 1796. Estimates for the 1797 procession, reviewed by General Lake, run from 10,000 to 30,000. By 1798 membership may have risen to 80,000, many of whom enrolled in the government sponsored Yeomanry. In Musgrave's view lower-class Protestants of the established church were "actuated by an invincible attachment to their king and country". Certainly, the totemic popular appeal of 'loyalty' and the blessings of the 'Protestant constitution' must not be underestimated. But Orangeism's greatest appeal was defensive and reactionary, the maintenance of 'Protestant Ascendancy' against the Catholic and republican challenge: *Croppies lie down!*

Ireland's unstable sectarian landscape accounts for both the vitality and the weakness of early Orangeism. Popular loyalism in Britain also

34

proclaimed its Protestant character, but, unlike Orangeism, the British associations' Protestantism reflected the religious affiliation of the majority of their countrymen. In Ireland inter-denominational strife and the size of the Catholic 'threat' drove thousands of lower-class Protestants into the Orange ranks. However, the same sectarian arithmetic permanently limited the movement's popular base. Still, the numbers were too impressive for a government confronted by a serious revolutionary challenge to ignore. Many an Orange Yeoman saw action in 1798.

Exclusively Protestant, the Orange Order was not, in its own view, sectarian. Its brand of Protestantism and anti-Catholicism (or, strictly speaking, anti-popery) was ostensibly political. All Protestants, whatever their doctrinal opinions were welcome to join the order, although in practice Episcopalians outnumbered Presbyterians. 'Popery' stood for tyranny and a 'disloyal' allegiance to a foreign prince. Catholics *per se* were entitled to their religious beliefs. Not that this theory prevented the United Irishmen from inventing an 'Orange extermination oath', or Catholics from believing it. Nor did refugees from the 'Armagh wreckings' harbour any doubts about the violent sectarianism of the Orangemen. The takeover of the Order by the gentry, in 1796-7, and Orangeism's counter-revolutionary ideology, seem to fit perfectly the Marxist interpretation of it as an instrument of class rule. That interpretation treats Orangeism, and sectarianism generally, as a variety of 'false consciousness', which divides the lower classes and sidetracks them from the pursuit of their 'objective' interests. General Knox, it is true, deliberately encouraged the Orangemen in their feud with the United Irishmen in Tyrone, but on balance the manipulation or false consciousness thesis (which not all Marxists subscribe to anyway) is patronising and crucially, fails to appreciate the self-generating capacity of popular loyalism. Rallying, as Musgrave put it, "round the altar and the throne, which were in imminent danger (the first Orangemen) united and stood forward ... unsupported by the great and powerful". The danger which Musgrave identified came from 'croppies', democrats and levellers, but lower class Orangemen also represented at least a potential threat. The men of property hijacked the movement in order to control it.●

James Napper Tandy

The Limits of Legislative Independence

Radicals, Reformers and Grattan's Parliament

By James Kelly

The reform of the Irish representative system was an issue in Irish politics for several decades before the United Irishmen sought to advance the question in the 1790s. Indeed, once it became clear following the 'Glorious Revolution' of 1688, which brought a limited constitutional monarchy into being in Britain, that ministers did not believe it appropriate to govern Ireland according to the same principles, a voice of protest quickly emerged. Many Irish Protestants were persuaded that as equal subjects under the crown, they deserved to enjoy exactly the same legal and constitutional rights as their fellow subjects resident in Britain.

James Kelly lectures in History in St Patrick's College, DCU, Drumcondra.
His biography of Henry Flood will be published in 1998.

Guided by this principle, the primary focus of their concerns in the first half of the 18th century was the level of control exerted by British politicians and officials over the Irish legislature. They objected most strongly to the authority accorded to the British Privy Council by Poynings's Law (1494), which allowed it to alter and veto legislation emanating from Ireland. Equally, they objected to the assertion by the British legislature, in the Declaratory Act of 1719, that it had the right to legislate for Ireland. In addition the fact that Irish subjects did not possess the protection of *habeas corpus* and that the law regulating the army and the terms upon which judges were appointed differed from that in Britain also rankled. But, irritated as they were by these manifestations of their subordination, Irish Protestants were unable to do much to mitigate their impact. Indeed, by introducing legislation which firstly reduced Catholic participation in politics and, from 1728, excluded Catholics from voting, they increased the ways in which the Irish parliament was an élitist body with limited powers. The exclusion of Catholics from the political process was a matter of satisfaction rather than concern for most Irish Protestants, until the 1790s.

In contrast to this, unease mounted (from mid-century) within the ranks of those who called themselves 'Patriots'. They perceived an undue influence exercised by the crown-appointed administration at Dublin Castle, through its use of political patronage - pensions and places in particular. They also sought to put an end to the practice whereby general elections were only held on the death of a monarch. The introduction of an Octennial Act in 1768, providing for general elections every eight years, represented an important advance in this respect. Attempts were made in the early 1770s by a number of reformers to advance a demand for the reform of the manner in which elections were conducted, but the outbreak of the American War of Independence shifted the political balance in favour of those Patriots who accorded greater priority to the reform of the Anglo-Irish constitutional and commercial *nexus*.

One of the keys to the ability of the Patriots to rally the Protestant nation behind their cause was the establishment of a countrywide network of Volunteer corps, a paramilitary force established to aid in the policing and defence of the country while the American war lasted. Their support greatly boosted the Patriots in parliament. As a result, they were enabled in 1779-80 to secure 'free trade', which involved the removal of commercial restraints on Irish commerce, and, in 1782, 'legislative independence' which involved the repeal of some of the legislative constraints on the Irish parliament and the dilution of others.

Better known as 'Grattan's parliament', the 'constitution of 1782' was seen by reform-minded middle class political activists as a most welcome development. Wolfe Tone expressed the positive attitude which was commonplace throughout the 1780s when he maintained that prior to 1782 Ireland had been "sunk to the subordination of an English county ... we had ceased to remember that we were a nation". But, stimulated by the example of the American colonists, Irish Protestants had exerted themselves during the late 1770s and early 1780s to break "the manacles" of "British ambition" and to rescue Ireland's "imperial crown" from "the felonious custody of arbitrary and jealous domination".

This was a rather exaggerated assessment of the import of the constitutional changes ratified in 1782, because for Tone, William Drennan, and those of comparable reformist or radical disposition who looked upon the alliance of Volunteers and Patriot MPs that achieved legislative independence with especial fondness, the constitution of 1782 was a beginning rather than an end. Like the Patriots in the House of Commons, they were exultant that the British government were obliged to repeal the offensive Declaratory Act. They were equally gratified that the British and Irish Privy Councils were deprived of the power to respite and amend the heads of bills emanating from both houses of the Irish parliament. But they wanted to build upon what had been achieved by taking up the reformist disposition they witnessed about them to create a momentum in favour of the fundamental structural reform of the Irish representative system.

This eagerness to continue reforming the political system was manifested in the summer and autumn of 1782 when Henry Flood's demand that the British parliament should not just simply repeal the Declaratory Act but renounce its claim to possess the right to legislate for Ireland was most firmly supported by middle-class Volunteer corps. The so-called 'renunciation' crisis was defused when the Westminster parliament recognized the legislative autonomy of the Irish parliament in the spring of 1783, by which date the middle-class activists and Volunteers whose involvement had contributed to the attainment of free trade and legislative independence were ready to set an agitation afoot whose purpose was to make the Irish legislature more representative.

The features of the representative system reformers believed most in need of reform were: the narrow franchise; the long duration of parliaments; and the disproportionate influence exercised by the controllers of the kingdom's boroughs, with their small electorates, who returned more than two-thirds of the House of Commons's 300 MPs. The enthusiastic endorsement by delegates from 304 Volunteer corps, assembled at Dungannon on 21st June 1782, of a resolution in favour of "the more equal representation of the people" and the support of the liberal press suggested that there was widespread popular support for reform. However, few had a clear idea of what specific reforms they desired.

With the objective of identifying what changes were most appropriate, information and advice were sought, by a committee of correspondence, from a range of prominent parliamentarians in Britain and Ireland. The response was disappointing. In spite of this delegates from 272 Ulster corps, gathered in Dungannon in September, approved resolutions in support of annual parliaments, the abolition of decayed boroughs and the redistribution of the seats thereby freed to "counties, cities and great towns", a secret ballot and the extension of the franchise to all Protestant males who satisfied a modest property qualification. The suggestion that Catholics should be enfranchised on the same terms was also discussed, but a decision on the matter was left to the Grand National Convention, which they urged should be held in Dublin in November 1783.

Because the priority of Henry Flood, the most popular Patriot of the time and the dominant influence at the Convention, was to devise a practicable plan of reform, such controversial matters as the enfranchisement of Catholics, a secret ballot and annual parliaments were put to one side when delegates gathered in November. The proposal for borough reform was also diluted. Despite this, when the plan was presented to the Irish House of Commons, a large majority of the MPs rejected it, on the grounds that they could not be expected "to receive propositions at the point of a bayonet" from a Volunteer assembly. This was a tenable position for the Irish parliament to take, but it was exposed for the pretence it was when they also rejected a reform bill which had been endorsed by freeholders in 22 counties the following March.

The implication of this was that the members of the élite which had dominated the Irish representative system for many decades were not prepared to allow the Protestant middle class access to the political process.

Angry and distressed, a number of radicals, headed by Napper Tandy, John Binns and the Ulster MP William Todd Jones, sought to continue the struggle by advancing a programme of radical reform which included Catholic enfranchisement. However, it was insufficiently well supported to overcome the entrenched resistance of established interests. Consequently, the issue of parliamentary reform disappeared off the political agenda for a number of years from 1785.

The categorical opposition of the Irish parliament to any reform of the representative system obviously disappointed its proponents. Many of those who supported reform responded by withdrawing from active political engagement or by pursuing other agendas in the second half of the 1780s. The response of Henry Flood, the parliamentarian most closely identified with reform, was more interesting.

Having observed at first hand the reassertion by the Dublin Castle executive, whose command of the government of Ireland was left unaltered by the constitutional changes implemented in 1782, of its dominance of the House of Commons, and having seen the supine conduct of MPs, who seemed content to leave the direction of Irish politics to managers sanctioned by the Lord Lieutenant and his superiors in London, Flood did not conceal his disillusionment with what, in 1786, he termed the 'drovers' and 'cattle' of College Green.

Like many Patriots and liberals, he had hoped that legislative independence signalled the start of a new era in responsible, participatory parliamentary government. But his dismissal of its proceedings in 1788 as a "lifeless, useless drama" indicated that, as far as he was concerned, the opposite had turned out to be the case.

Flood did not turn his back on parliamentary politics, but the fact that he, the parliamentarian *par excellence*, was prepared to question the appropriateness of a crown-appointed executive representing Ireland in negotiations in which Britain had an interest suggested that other, more stern, criticisms of the narrowness and limitations of the Irish political system might not be long in following.

Flood's evident reluctance to attribute the deficiencies of the Irish parliament to the incompleteness of the constitutional reforms of 1782 attested to the continuing pride in what had been achieved. It is significant, for example, that the Whig Club, founded in 1790 by Grattan and his allies to advance liberal politics, and which included Tone, Tandy and other radicals among its members, defined the preservation of the Irish constitution as settled in 1688 and 1782 as "the great object of the society". It also deemed the connection with Britain "sacred and indissoluble". The Whigs were not defenders of the *status quo* for all that, but it soon became clear that the programme of patronage reforms they sought to advance in the early 1790s offered little to the middle classes, for whom admission to a reformed representative system was essential if it was to retain their respect and allegiance. Tone said as much in his vastly influential tract, *An argument on behalf of the Catholics of Ireland* (Dublin 1791), where he described the "revolution of 1782" as a "most bungling imperfect business" that left "three fourths of our countrymen slaves as it found them".

As Tone's reactions testify, the outbreak of revolution in France provided middle-class reformers with just the stimulus they needed to reanimate the campaign for parliamentary reform which had fizzled out so ingloriously in 1785. Stimulated by the success of the French radicals in overturning what was widely perceived to be one of the most autocratic systems in Europe, and by the belief that a "complete and radical reform in the representation" was the key to the creation of responsive, efficient and principled government in Ireland, they determined to advance an even more radical plan than they had favoured in the 1780s. Their programme now included Catholic relief and the diminution of the influence of the British government over Irish affairs as well as parliamentary reform, but the latter was the issue they felt they could press with most confidence.

The United Irishmen was the organisation which, from its foundation late in 1791, most assertively embraced the challenge of advancing this reformist programme. Given their close links with the parliamentary reform movement of the 1780s - leading members like Napper Tandy, William Drennan, Wolfe Tone and Hamilton Rowan had agitated for parliamentary reform in the 1780s - and their admiration for the Volunteers, it is not entirely surprising that the strategy they adopted to advance the cause of reform was essentially the same as that adopted in the early 1780s to secure legislative independence. They calculated that this was the most likely means to channel the necessary public and political support to convince MPs to reform the system of representation.

This could not happen, of course, without the active support of a dynamic Volunteer organisation, and since the Volunteers were but a pale shadow of the organization that had proved so influential in 1779 and 1782, attempts were made to reanimate the volunteering spirit. This was a formidable challenge, but, encouraged by the evidence that support for reform was strong in Ulster, it was decided to take William Drennan's suggestion and give the demand for reform coherence and direction by holding a Convention of parochial delegates at Dungannon in February 1793. Though thoughtful strategists might have anticipat· 1 that this rather blatant attempt to repeat the formula which had produced legislative independence in 1782 was unlikely to succeed, the moderate nature of the resolutions that were approved offered some grounds for hope. The delegates affirmed their attachment to the British constitution, as well as advocating the disfranchisement of boroughs, the extension of the franchise equally to people of all religions, equal constituencies and frequent elections.

Many United Irishmen did not believe the Convention's resolutions went far enough but, despite this, most accepted William Drennan's assessment that they were "prudent and useful". The fact that a number of prominent Irish Whigs were known to be in favour of the plan was also encouraging because the efforts of Tandy and leading Unitedmen in Dublin to form a new Volunteer corps, along the lines of the French National Guard, had been deemed illegal by the Privy Council in December 1792. Unwilling to forfeit their primary means of rallying support and bringing pressure to bear on the authorities, the United Irish leadership sought to press on with their campaign, but with the first display of official firmness, their resolve dissipated and this effectively put an end to this attempt to revitalise volunteering. This was a serious setback, and northern radicals did not conceal their disappointment at the outcome. However, when their own resolve was tested, by the intervention of the authorities in March, both Belfast and Coleraine Volunteers proved no more defiant than had been their Dublin equivalents.

In view of the failure of the United Irishmen to engender a powerful public campaign, the task of progressing parliamentary reform shifted to the combination of Whig and Patriot MPs who were well disposed towards reform. They were not without optimism that their moderate proposals for extending the boundaries of boroughs, for increasing county and populous constituencies from two to three seaters and for broadening the electorate would prove acceptable, but the bulk of MPs were as resistant as ever. They were unpersuaded by Grattan's claim that his moderate plan should be supported because it would strengthen the role of "the propertied part of the community" in government. Convinced by events in France that it was dangerous to tinker with what they still identified as the best constitution devised by man, they rejected the plan of reform, by a decisive margin, during the 1793 session.

Despite these setbacks, both the parliamentary proponents of moderate reform and the United Irish advocates of more fundamental change determined to press on. Having taken extensive soundings, the United Irishmen finally produced a formal statement of their position in the winter of 1793-4. In this they advocated annual parliaments, the payment of representatives, 300 equal electoral districts, adult male suffrage, *viva voce* voting, and one day polls.

This, inevitably, was a more radical proposal than that advanced by the Whigs in the Irish parliament, and it indicated that the United Irishmen had not given up hope on the Irish parliament. At the same time, the fact that, unlike the Whigs, they no longer trumpeted the constitution of 1782 indicated that the confidence they had expressed in that settlement during the 1780s had been dissipated by the unregenerate resistance of the legislature, as currently constituted, to the legitimate aspirations of the people to be represented. This proved well justified since further attempts to advance parliamentary reform during the 1794 and subsequent sessions also foundered on the rocks of established interests. As a consequence many United Irishmen concluded in the mid-1790s that they had little alternative but to embrace revolutionary tactics to secure the reform of the Irish representative system.

The uncompromising resistance of the Irish executive and of a majority of MPs to the reform of the Irish parliament was the main reason for the increasing disenchantment of revolutionaries and reformers with parliamentary government in Ireland in the 1790s. It did not disillusion them with the idea of parliamentary government however. It is clear from the pamphlet, *The Union doctrine or poor man's cathechism*, published in the late 1790s, that though the United Irishmen's vision for Ireland then differed fundamentally from moderate Whigs as well as ultra-conservatives, all were agreed on the centrality of parliamentary government. This is significant because it suggests that if the constitutional reforms implemented in 1782 had been followed by the internal reform of the representative system constitutionalism might have accommodated the demands for change that arose in the 1790s and thereby obviated the need for recourse to revolution.

Further Reading:
RB McDowell, *Ireland in the age of imperialism and revolution 1760-1801* (Oxford, 1979).
James Kelly, 'Parliamentary reform in Irish politics 1760-90' in D Dickson, D Keogh and K Whelan (eds), *The United Irishmen; republicanism, radicalism and rebellion* (Dublin, 1993), pp 74-87.
Marianne Elliott, *Wolfe Tone: prophet of Irish independence* (Yale, 1989). ●

Daniel O'Connell

The Act of Union
A Solution for All Time or Doomed From the Outset?

by Jacqueline Hill

The Act of Union that came into force on January 1st 1801 formally brought to an end the Kingdom of Ireland, by uniting it with that of Great Britain to form a single 'United Kingdom of Great Britain and Ireland'. The Irish parliament ceased to exist, and Irish representation was transferred to Westminster.

Jacqueline Hill lectures in Modern History at NUI Maynooth, and her book *From Patriots to Unionists: Dublin Civic Politics and Irish Protestant Patriotism 1660-1840* appeared in 1997.

Although the union was intended to last 'for ever', some of its immediate provisions were overturned during the 19th century, for instance, the Church of Ireland was disestablished in 1869 and in the aftermath of the 1916 rising the Government of Ireland Act of 1920 restored representation to Ireland, albeit creating *two* subordinate Irish parliaments rather than one. That Act held out the prospect of a single parliament for the whole island (article $2^{(1)}$), but the War of Independence and the Anglo-Irish Treaty of 1921 saw the 26-counties opt out of these arrangements and take on a new existence as the Irish Free State.

Under the Treaty the king was recognised only

in virtue of the common citizenship of Ireland with Great Britain and ... membership of the group of nations forming the British commonwealth of nations. (Article 4).

Within three decades the declaration of an Irish Republic saw the last vestiges of union disappear in the South as the Republic left the Commonwealth. In Northern Ireland, however, the union (as modified by the Government of Ireland Act) has continued, although the Stormont parliament was abolished in 1973, since when Northern Ireland has been ruled directly from London.

Why was the Act of Union introduced? To historians writing in the nationalist tradition the answer seemed straightforward. For the Young Irelander John Mitchel it was the prospect in the 1790s of Irishmen of all creeds coming together that alarmed the British government (*The History of Ireland ... in Two Volumes*, 4th edn., vol. 2, p 87, James Duffy, Dublin). A century later the explanation given by PS O'Hegarty was much the same (*A History of Ireland under the Union*, pp 3-4, Kraus, New York, 1969). Recent accounts are more likely to stress the long gestation of the union issue, commencing in the 17th century.

A short-lived legislative union promulgated in the Cromwellian era proved unsatisfactory to both England and Ireland, but, following the Williamite wars of the 1690s Irish Protestants, who had just been restored to power, were anxious to obtain a union for reasons of trade, religion, and security. This was a period when a perceived threat of 'universal monarchy' seemed to emanate from Louis XIV's France: Protestantism was being pressed back into the northern periphery of Europe, and representative assemblies, such as the French Estates General, were being undermined by growing royal power.

One solution to the danger from "popery and arbitrary power" (as contemporaries put it) was to consider forming Protestant leagues and unions. Such a course was much discussed in Ireland and in Scotland. But although the Irish parliament passed resolutions in 1703 and in 1709 in favour of union with England, it was the Scots who, in 1707, obtained one. Not all Scots were in favour of union, but farmers and merchants expected to gain from trading directly with England's overseas colonies. The prospect of having to share such opportunities with the Scots was not appealing in England, but the security issue, in a period of prolonged European war, was persuasive. Security hinged on the succession to the English throne. When it became clear that James II's daughters, Mary and Anne, were unlikely to have any living children the English parliament decided to settle the crown on a remote (but Protestant) branch of the royal family, the electors of Hanover, rather than accept the return of a Catholic dynasty.

The Scots, angry over England's failure to back their commercial projects, threatened to take an independent line over the succession. In order to avoid such a prospect, the London government backed the idea of an English and Scottish legislative union, which duly admitted the Scots to all the benefits of free trade with English colonies, while respecting the official status of the Presbyterian church and the Scottish legal system.

Irish Protestants were too few and too divided between dissenters, Presbyterians for the most part, and members of the established church, the Church of Ireland, even to toy with the idea of backing a Jacobite restoration. On the contrary, almost as soon as the English parliament had voted to settle the crown on the Hanoverians the Irish parliament endorsed the decision. It therefore lacked the bargaining power of the Scots, and there was no inducement for a London government to grant commercial benefits to Ireland, as the price of a legislative union. Consequently, during the 18th century, the Irish parliament remained in existence, and the London government continued to exercise control through the appointment of the Irish executive, based in Dublin Castle.

In the absence of union, relations between Ireland and Britain in the 18th century were for the most part smooth. Although a right to legislate for Ireland was formally asserted by the British parliament in 1720 (a similar claim was to be made in respect of the American colonies in 1766) the claim was exercised with caution. Acts of 1663 (restricting the importation of Irish cattle into Britain) and of 1699 (prohibiting the export of Irish woollens, except to England) continued to cause bad feeling, but Ireland did derive some benefits from the English colonial empire, especially from the trade in provisions.

Most clashes arose not from legislation imposed from London but from executive actions, such as the 'Wood's halfpence affair', which concerned the granting of a patent to coin money for Ireland. However, resentment over the fact that the Scots had obtained a union while Ireland had not, continued to be expressed, notably by Jonathan Swift in 'The Story of the Injured Lady', (*Prose Works*, vol. 7, pp 97-103, ed. Temple Scott, London, 1905).

The patriotism displayed by Irish Protestants continued to have unionist overtones down to about the middle of the 18th century. But by then the growth of the Irish economy and the dimming of any prospect of a Jacobite restoration combined to put the issue in a new light. This was a period when middling ranks of Protestants in town and country began to make their voices heard within the political system, and they were particularly keen to safeguard and promote economic progress. Unlike the aristocracy and greater gentry, these Protestants had little hope of influencing policy in London, so to them the Irish parliament took on a special importance. Talk of legislative union became anathema, and from 1759 onwards riots were apt to break out in Dublin at any rumour that government might be contemplating such a step.

The crisis posed by the American War of Independence prompted the formation of the Volunteers, whose rank-and-file represented mainly the Protestant middle classes. They called for free trade (the right to trade directly with Britain's colonies) which was granted in 1779-80. To safeguard this concession the Volunteers then demanded legislative independence, requiring the British parliament to abandon its claim to make laws binding on Ireland. In this limited form (the Irish executive continued to be appointed in London) independence was conceded in 1782-3, giving rise to 'Grattan's parliament'.

Meanwhile in England resistance (on commercial grounds) to an Irish union had been weakening since mid-century. Union was actually commended by the new economic thinkers such as Adam Smith, who considered that the idea of commercial rivalry between the two countries was outmoded. With the successful Scottish example in mind British ministers in the American revolutionary era began to look more favourably on union as a means of stabilising relations between the two countries. But nothing could be done while Irish Protestant feeling remained strongly anti-unionist.

The extremist course taken by the French revolution after 1790 prompted the British government to try to mobilise as much counter-revolutionary potential as possible, in order to shore up the British system of parliamentary monarchy. The arguments of Edmund Burke, who commended the Catholic church as a conservative and stabilising force, became more cogent as the church in France fell victim to the revolution. Against this background the London government conferred political rights on the Catholics of Québec, and began to consider doing the same for Irish Catholics. But although most Irish Protestants had accepted the relaxation of the penal laws relating to land and education, fears about "popery and arbitrary power" were still present, and the issue of political rights for Catholics, in a country with a Catholic majority, was so sensitive that it had scarcely figured on the political agenda, except for a small, mostly Presbyterian, fringe.

Heedless of these sensitivities, the government pressed its agenda on the Dublin authorities, with the result that very extensive political rights were granted to Irish Catholics in 1792-3 (only the right to sit in parliament and to hold certain higher posts in the army and public service were withheld).

Protestants were deeply divided, and it quickly emerged that in the absence of reform of the franchise and of local government it would be difficult for Catholics to exercise all these new rights. By this time Britain was at war with revolutionary France and the climate was not conducive to further reform. Apart from this, the Irish countryside was being seriously disturbed by the quasi-revolutionary activities of the mainly Catholic Defenders. Against this background some Protestants took a radical course and joined the United Irishmen, which soon developed separatist overtones; others lined up behind Henry Grattan and the Whigs, calling for further reform; yet others adopted a strongly loyalist stance. These internal divisions in what had hitherto been a relatively cohesive Protestant élite facilitated the 1798 rebellion.

By 1798 Ireland appeared to government to be dangerously unstable, while for many Protestants concern over sectarian overtones in the rebellion, plus the admission of Catholics to political rights, served to weaken their former hostility to union. Nevertheless, it seems clear (*The Fall and Rise of the Irish Nation*, pp 252-9, Thomas Bartlett, Gill & Macmillan, Dublin, 1992) that government would not have been able to persuade Irish MPs to accept a union had it not been for the disposition of Irish Catholics. Although Dublin Catholics proved an exception, most Catholics backed union as the best way of securing the repeal of the remaining penal laws ('Catholic emancipation'), and as a safeguard against the excesses of the Orange Order, which was founded in 1795. Catholics had had the vote since 1793, so they were able to make their influence felt, and (after government had smoothed the way with financial compensation and other inducements) the Irish parliament voted in 1800 to accept a union.

It has often been argued that the union between Britain and Ireland was doomed from the outset, because of the failure to grant Catholic emancipation despite the tacit assurances given to Catholic bishops and others in the prelude to union. Daniel O'Connell himself suggested otherwise: if emancipation had been granted at any time during the first two decades of the union, it would have been regarded as a boon ('Address to the Catholics of Ireland', *Dublin Journal*, 6th January 1819). As it turned out, emancipation was not granted before the unprecedented mobilisation of the Catholic masses through the Catholic Association, set up in 1824. Even so, there was a good deal of Protestant support for emancipation. But few Protestants supported repeal of the union, and it was O'Connell's decision, following the winning of emancipation, to proceed at once to campaign for repeal that saw Irish politics take on their largely sectarian format, with Catholics (by and large) adopting a repeal and home rule position and Protestants (for the most part) backing the union.

No assessment of the working of the union can be attempted here, though it may be pointed out that there are 'malign' and 'benign' versions of the Irish experience. Adherents of the former view are apt to stress the disaster of the famine, emigration, and sectarianism; those who tend to the latter point to famine relief, Victorian reforms (such as the land acts) and attempts to combat sectarianism.

But one aspect of Anglo-Irish relations under the union may be touched on by way of conclusion: Ireland's liability to contribute to United Kingdom expenditure, which was set out in the Act of Union (article 7).

Britain's involvement in the Napoleonic wars, which lasted until 1815, had the effect of greatly increasing that expenditure. From time to time, particularly after income tax was extended to Ireland in 1853, nationalist politicians alleged that Ireland was overtaxed and there was some merit in their case. Although, for example, it has been estimated that for the year of 1870 the share of Ireland's national income taken by taxation was the same as that taken in Britain (and tax rates were uniform throughout the United Kingdom) the fact was that taxation fell disproportionately heavily on the poorer classes, and the Irish population was poorer than that of Britain.

In relative terms, Ireland's importance as a source of revenue did not rank anywhere near that of India, but it was more useful than Canada, or the Australian colonies, which paid nothing towards the servicing of the national debt or to the upkeep of the British army or navy.

However, from the 1860s onwards, Irish revenue was declining, because of the growing cost of services, and with the introduction of old age pensions in 1909 Ireland actually became a financial liability to Britain, until this trend was reversed by the first world war (see *A New History of Ireland*, vol. 5, ch. 32, ed. WE Vaughan, Oxford University Press, 1989).●

Kilmainham Gaol

Inchicore Road, Dublin 8

One of the largest unoccupied gaols in Europe, covering some of the most heroic and tragic events in Ireland's emergence as a modern nation, from the 1780s to the 1920s.
Attractions include exhibitions and an audio-visual show.
Access by guided tour only.

ADMISSION: Adults £3.00; Group & Senior Citizens £2.00; Child/Student £1.25; Family Rate £7.50.
HOURS OF OPENING: April - September: Daily 9.30 to 16.45; October - March: Monday to Friday 9.30 to 16.00; Closed Saturdays; Sundays 10 to 16.45.

Dúchas The Heritage Service

Theobald Wolfe Tone
Irish Republicanism
and Separatism

by Thomas Bartlett

In his speech at his court martial in November 1798, Wolfe
Tone averred, "From my earliest youth I have regarded the
connexion between Ireland and Great Britain as the curse of
the Irish nation; and felt convinced that whilst it lasted, this
country could never be free nor happy."

Thomas Bartlett is Professor of Modern Irish History at the NUI, University College Dublin,
and is currently editing a work on the life of Wolfe Tone, to be published in 1998.

However, his assertion of a life-long commitment to separatism has received short shrift from his biographers: Frank MacDermot's tart rebuttal of his claim - "the facts furnish all the comment that is necessary" - was later amplified by Tom Dunne, who cast Tone as an unanchored misfit, an 'outsider', who longed to find "an acceptable career, a meaningful role, some fulfilment of the expectations natural to a member of the colonial elite", and who, through "alienation and despair" became a separatist and a revolutionary. Marianne Elliott, too, claims that Tone's conversion to separatism was almost wholly a product of his American exile of 1795 and was thus not only comparatively late in the day, but represented "a case of necessity as much as choice", and was even "an accident of character as much as of timing". As with Tone's separatism, so too his republican credentials have been called into question. Dunne points to Tone's enthusiasm for colonial enterprises in the South Seas, his unabashed admiration for French aggression, his loathing of the new American republic, even his fondness and sympathy for both George III of England and Louis XVI of France, and concludes that such attributes hardly seem in keeping with the common perception of true republican principles.

Again, Elliott has noted Tone's lack of interest in cultural matters - Irish music, history, language and literature apparently left him cold; while Dunne has commented on his patronising attitude towards Catholics in general, but towards especially 'Poor Pat', the prisoner of war, easily bought for a bottle of wine and a tumble with a *fille de joie*. Tone, remarks Dunne, may have turned his back on the Protestant Ascendancy, but he did not - could not? - reject the outlook of easy cultural superiority that was inseparable from it.

Such provocative insights invite a further reflection on Tone's thought and achievements; it may be found on examination that his claim to novelty as well as consistency are rather stronger than either Elliott or Dunne maintain.

At the outset, it is clear that Tone's republicanism must be firmly located in the 18th century, and judged by the criteria of the time, rather than by the standards of later generations. But what did republicanism mean at that time? Republicans espoused contrary views as to whether a republican form of government was suitable to a small country or to a large one; whether a republic would have a propensity for peace or for war; and contradictory viewpoints were voiced on the question of whether a republic should foster commerce or seek to restrain economic growth; and there was little agreement on such weighty matters as equality and representation. Nor indeed was there a consensus on the question of whether a republic had to adopt a specific form of government. Provided the 'common weal' was pursued, and 'commonwealth' was for a long time the usual translation from the Latin *res publica*, there was much scope for discussion. Thus, in the 18th century a republic was by no means seen as being incompatible with monarchy. Machiavelli, the Renaissance philosopher, writing in the early 16th century, was both Machiavelli, the republican and author of the *Discourses*, and also Machiavelli, the monarchist and author of *The Prince*, and the classic republican texts since his time had been equally ambivalent on this question.

Republicanism since the 16th century, wrote JGA Pocock, was "more a language than a programme" and the vocabulary was one of protest, of resistance to tyrants, combining a hatred of corruption with a quest for civic virtue. It was generally assumed that political virtue and civic virtue would be found most readily, though not exclusively, in a country whose citizens had the predominant part in the election or selection of their magistrate, prince or king; and for this reason, republicans everywhere sought to give a preponderant role to the people. Wherever the people had little or no say, either because of despotism or corruption, republicans were generally found to be seeking a return to some golden age or, more often, advocating parliamentary reform.

Moreover, there was universal recognition of the spirit which ought to infuse a republic. From Niccolo Machiavelli to Tom Paine and including such 17th and 18th century writers as Milton, Harrington, Montesquieu and Gibbon, republican writers agreed that "public virtue is the only foundation of republics". This moral dimension to republicanism came before everything else: with it, the common good was promoted and liberty protected; without it, chaos and corruption reigned. Republicanism therefore constituted a moral challenge to its adherents, placing a heavy burden on them to live up to its promise.

Where does Tone stand in this brief examination of 18th century republicanism? Tone never claimed to be an ideologue and, as Dunne and Elliott have noted, he was far from being a systematic thinker.

Hubert Butler in his elegant essay on Tone, remarks that "what made Tone great was that he had no ideology". That said, there are good enough grounds for arguing that Tone had been, from an early date, a thorough-going republican; at any rate, he was as much a republican as those whose credentials in that respect have never been questioned.

In the first instance, Tone's language was unmistakably republican, filled with notions of resistance to tyrants, opposition to hereditary aristocracies and replete with aspirations to end corruption and promote virtue. In these respects, we can see Tone's indebtedness to the commonwealthman or republican rhetoric associated with such 18th century writers as William Molesworth, Francis Hutcheson and John Toland. Tone's faith in parliamentary reform - "with a parliament thus reformed everything is easy; without it nothing can be done" - was wholly republican and recognisably within the republican tradition.

His social conservatism - not as strong as is claimed - was equally in keeping with republican thought as it had developed since the Renaissance. Nor does Tone's preference for 'strong' government call into question his republicanism. His remark that while there would be "just and reasonable liberty of the press ... libels and calumnies" on the government would be severely published, was unexceptional, for libel laws - and sumptuary laws and price controls - were part of the republican agenda at that time. Equally, Tone's admiration for the martial virtues, even to the extent of proposing a military colony in the South Seas, should best be seen not as the negation of republicanism but (as Marianne Elliott reminds us) rather as evidence of "a continuing mesmerisation with the military vigour of ancient (republican) Rome."

Tone's republicanism was certainly eclectic; but this was because republicanism was itself eclectic at that time. Only when 20th century criteria of republicanism are applied to Tone is he found wanting. Viewed amongst his contemporaries, Tone is seen for what he was - a recognisable 18th century republican.

In a similar fashion, Tone's contribution to the modern separatist ideal - that Ireland could exist separate from Britain and independent of all other countries - may have been underestimated. Certainly, separatism, in the sense of merely severing the links with Britain, had been tossed around in Irish political discourse for several hundred years: but it had been very much a minority demand, typically voiced by religious exiles marooned on the continent. Rarely, if ever, until the late 18th century, was it envisaged that Ireland could go it alone. Separation from England was commonly seen as a necessary prelude to connection with Spain or France. Admittedly, some English politicians were convinced that they could hear the authentic separatist note in the rhetoric of the Anglo-Irish opposition spokesmen of the early and mid 18th century. Why English observers should have considered separatism to be an element within Irish patriotism is something of a puzzle. It is possible that anxiety over the 'true' nature of the Anglo-Irish connection - was Ireland a colony, conquered province or sister kingdom? - played a part here, and so too surely, did the English view of the Anglo-Irish relationship as being identical to that between a mother and its child, with Ireland being cast in the role of dependent child. Implicit in this child-colony/mother-country relationship was the threat that the 'child' would one day grow up and seek independence and separation.

Moreover, there were undoubtedly fears in the 1770s that the secession of the American colonies might prove contagious; and it was surely in recognition of this threat that, from the 1770s on, there emerged a distinct constituency in English politics which saw a legislative union, on financial, political and strategic grounds, as the ultimate solution to the problem of Anglo-Irish relations. Unionism fed on the fear of separation; and that fear, already heightened by the winning of the 'Constitution of 1782', which conceded a quasi independence to the Irish parliament, was further fuelled by the failure in the 1780s to repair that dangerously flawed 'final settlement'.

But unionism also bred separatism, for the more talk there was of union, and the more that option was couched in the black or white, either or, terms of 'union or separation', then the more the idea of separation came to be discussed.

Where does Tone stand in the separatist tradition? Clearly he did not invent the idea: separatism was, if not implicit, then concealed somewhere in the colonial nationalism espoused in Ireland in the 18th century. In any case, after the secession of the American colonies, separatism as a political concept was in the air. Nor need we accept Tone's claim made in France in 1796 that he had been a separatist from his earliest days. That said, there was a separatist note to his writings, a separatist logic to his actions and a willingness to embrace the separatist option that together marked Tone out as the first Irish separatist.

Some years after its publication, Tone claimed that in his pamphlet *Spanish War!* (1790) he had "advanced the question of separatism with scarcely any reserve", though in fact overtly separatist sentiments were well concealed in this tract. Tone's demand for a national flag, navy and army could have been accommodated within the existing Anglo-Irish relationship. On the other hand, such appendages were the usual ones for fully sovereign states and it is clear that Tone was in effect, attempting to move the issue of national independence onto the agenda of Irish politics. But he moved very cautiously. In his *Argument on behalf of the Catholics of Ireland* (1791), he started to answer those who claimed that "Ireland is unable to exist as an independent state", but then apparently, he decided that it was not yet time to broach that subject. He confined his views to private letters such as that he wrote to his great friend Thomas Russell, in July 1791, in which he declared that as "for separation ... I give it to you and your friends as my most decided opinion that such an event would be the regeneration to this country", but at the same time he admitted that "that opinion is for the present too hardy".

This letter was used by the Earl of Clare, Lord Chancellor of Ireland, to denounce all United Irishmen as out and out separatists.

Tone's outraged denial in the *Freeman's Journal* that he was in fact a separatist was hedged with so many conditions as to be quite unconvincing. "I for one do not wish to break the connection", he noted piously,

> provided it can be, as I am sure it can, preserved consistently with the honour, the interests and the happiness of Ireland. If I were, on the other hand, satisfied that it could not be so preserved, I would hold it a sacred duty to endeavour by all possible means to break it.

Even at this stage, Tone surely knew that the interests of Ireland would receive short shrift from England during the war with Revolutionary France; that after 1793 the only alternative, as Clare never tired of declaring, was union or separation, not union or reform. Reform to Dublin Castle was merely another word for separation.

It was Tone's realisation that such was the case, that the republicanism which he sought could only be achieved through breaking the link, that drove him along the road to separation.

So long as the connection with England remained, Tone believed that his republican ideals could not be realised. It was, in the end, he believed, English connection, not Irish division, that thwarted the achievment of republicanism: and the English connection had, therefore, to go.

Further reading
MacDermot, *Tone and his Times*
Tom Dunne, *Theobald Wolfe Tone: Colonial Outsider*, (Cork, 1982)
Tone, *Life*, i, pp 499
Tone, *Life*, ii, pp 64,
Hubert Butler, *Wolfe Tone and the Common Name of Irishman*, (Dublin, 1985) ●

The Women of 1798
Representations and Realities

by Dáire Keogh

When the tyrant's hand was laid
Upon the true and brave.
In the tender pride of womanhood
The true rose to help and save.
('Leo', John Keegan Casey 1846-70).

Dáire Keogh lectures in the history department of St Patrick's College, Drumcondra, DCU.
He is co-editor of the book *The Women of 1798*, Four Courts Press, 1998.

No aspect of the 1798 rebellion has been quite so neglected as that of the role of women in the events of that year. Contemporaries drew upon their experience, but for the most part the women's voices were smothered beneath the partisan priorities of the commentators.

There was little enthusiasm in the immediate aftermath of the rebellion for an accurate record of events, since both the loyalists and the vanquished attempted to play down the politicisation of the 1790s. The former sought to interpret the rising as a *jacquerie*, or popish plot, while the latter attempted to minimise their culpability, representing themselves as 'reluctant rebels', or moderating elements, in a spontaneous rebellion provoked by unrelenting terror.

Within this scenario it was difficult to accommodate the totality of the women's experience and such priorities contributed to their depoliticisation and relegation to secondary roles. This tendency is immediately apparent in the great loyalist history of the insurrection, Sir Richard Musgrave's mammoth *Memoirs of the Irish rebellion* (Dublin, 1801). This account characterises the women as victims, mourners or raving fanatics. Many of the depositions reproduced recall their sufferings and few are more moving than that of Elizabeth Dobbyn of Old Court, County Wexford, whose husband and two sons were amongst the one hundred killed in the atrocity at Scullabogue.

In contrast Musgrave represents the rebel women as bloodthirsty extremists, devoid of the natural inclinations of their sex. While the flames engulfed the prisoners at Scullabogue one woman called out, "Do they want water? Give them poison." When prisoners on Vinegar Hill pleaded for mercy, Mary Redmond insisted they be put to death, while the massacre on Wexford Bridge is attributed to the influence of Margery Dixon "whose thirst for protestant blood was insatiable" and who urged the rebels to save their ammunition and "to give the prisoners plenty of piking".

As well as the partisan inspiration such accounts drew from, these interpretations were due in part to 18th century attitudes, which made a rigid distinction between male and female roles. It is an irony of the Enlightenment that the *philosophes*, through their reflection on the question of gender, perpetuated the notion of women as being inferior to men. Definitions of femininity were altered, but the effect remained the same: women were excluded from the public realm, refused the vote and the right to serve as jurors.

Such restrictions were an institutionalisation of attitudes which could hardly accommodate the notion of women as politicised rebels.

Mary Wollstonecraft compared this denial of rights to women to the condition of slaves. Yet the United Irishmen, for all their lofty talk of liberty refused to entertain the possibility of the admission of women to the political process. This, however, did not mean that women were uninvolved, despite their exclusion from the United Irish programme. As in France, where women's participation was necessary to the success of the revolution, Ireland's 'rebel daughters' played an active role in the radicalism of the decade. Many took the secondary 'oath of secrecy'. A Society of United Irishwomen had been established by 1796.

There were prominent female activists like Mrs Oliver Bond whose Trojan efforts in propagating the United cause were brought to the attention of the Dublin Castle authorities. Others shared Pamela Fitzgerald's role, acting as couriers. There were those who, like Mary Anne McCracken, sought to convince men of the necessity of embracing women's rights.

In the rebellion itself women also made a significant contribution. For the most part they acted in a supporting role, but there is evidence that they were active in the field. One contemporary illustration survives, which shows "the lovely and accomplished Miss Redmond, leader of the rebels, on her charger at the battle of Wexford". Yet after the rebellion the contribution of women was largely ignored; as Thomas Bartlett observed, "women could be symbols or model or victim but ... the role of actor, activist or combatant - in a political context -was denied them."

In the second half of the 19th century, however, as the centenary drew near, gestures were made to incorporate the women of '98 into the rash of literature and ballads which marked the celebrations. For the most part these accounts were based on slender evidence. While it might be argued that the women's memory had lived on in folklore, many of the legends appear contrived and follow the universal patterns of heroism. Mary Doyle, for example, the heroine of New Ross, receives mention in Thomas Cloney's *Narrative* (1832), for her part in saving a cannon for the rebels, but her reputation is largely based upon William Rooney's depiction of her urging on the United army with a wave of her scythe:

But a figure rose before us, 'twas a girl's fragile frame,
And among the fallen soldiers, there she walked with eyes aflame,
And her voice rang o'er the clamour, like a trumpet o'er the sea,
'Whoso dares to die for Ireland, let him come and follow me!

The North Leinster campaign had its heroine, too, but in the case of
Molly Weston, evidence is scant and her reputation is based primarily
on the records of Patrick Archer the chronicler of Fingal. A native of
Worganstown, near Oldtown, County Meath, she was alleged to have
been active in recruiting United Irish members prior to the rebellion.
Once the fighting began, she rode into battle upon a white horse
dressed in green and braid, sporting a plume in her green cocked hat.
Her bravery was renowned and legend recalls how, taking charge of a
field piece, she inflicted heavy casualties upon the Reagh Fencibles.

In a similar way the story of Betsy Grey of Granshaw, County
Down, has been enshrined in ballads, verse and WG Lyttle's novel,
Betsy Gray, or the Hearts of Down (1886). Celebrated as 'Ulster's
Joan of Arc', tradition recalls how she fought at the Battle of
Ballynahinch alongside her brother and her lover, William Boal.
Mounted on a white horse she inspired the men, leading them on with
a green flag, or, in some accounts a sword, until she was cut down by
a party of the Hillsborough Yeomanry Cavalry.

Apart from this stereotypical depiction of the women of 1798 their
memory was also tailored to fit the temper of the time and the Catholic
Nationalism which dominated the commemorations. There was,
therefore, a selective revival of folkloric traditions which reinforced
earlier accounts stressing their femininity and confining women's
participation to a supporting role. The account of Paddy Roarke is
typical of this development. Captured at the battle of Oulart, he was
offered his life in return for information. Bravely, his mother
intervened, urging him to: "Die like a man, and never be an informer."
The poor woman knelt on the street of Bunclody, bared her breast, and
called out: "Now, you murdering Yeomen, shoot me and let me die
with my son."

Likewise, the less attractive aspects of women's activities in 1798
were summarily dismissed. Accordingly, Bridget 'Croppy Biddy'
Dolan, an active rebel turned informer, was castigated as a common
prostitute and libidinous wretch.

This 'nationalisation' reached its climax with the publication of Helena Concannon's *Women of 'Ninety Eight* (1919), written in the context of the Anglo-Irish War. This was an old fashioned history in which the secondary role of the subjects was implied by chapter titles like 'The Mothers of '98' and 'The Wives of '98' which were as likely intended to be an inspiration for her contemporaries as a history of the rebellion. Yet, for all this, Concannon's work represented a significant contribution and has until this year remained the unique study of the subject. Her work is now joined by a collection of essays, edited by Dáire Keogh and Nicholas Furlong, entitled simply *The Women of 1798* (Four Courts Press, Dublin, 1998), which attempts to redress the neglect of an important aspect of women's history and illustrate what has long been suspected: the involvement of women not alone as symbol, victim and observer, but as activist, combatant and loyalist in Ireland's attempted revolution. ●

Thomas Russell

A United Irishman from Wexford

The Wexford Republic of June 1798

A Story Hidden from History

by Kevin Whelan

In the epic story of the 1798 rebellion, some of the more significant events can become obscured by superficially more exciting incidents, such as the battles themselves. One such event, the efforts by the United Irishmen to create a Republican and democratic government in Wexford town while it was under their control, has been totally ignored, while historians like Pakenham have dwelt at length on the Wexford bridge massacre. Yet, this brave, innovative but ultimately doomed attempt to create a genuinely new form of democratic participation in municipal organisation was one of the most striking features of the whole rebellion, even though it did not lodge in the popular imagination in the same way in which more flamboyant episodes did.

Kevin Whelan is a historical geographer and Dublin Director of Notre Dame University. He has published numerous articles on 1798.

Ignored by historians, almost completely unknown by Wexford town people, uncelebrated in song or story, the 'Wexford Republic' richly deserves to be inserted again into the mainstream of discussion of 1798. Given the disorder, chaos and pandemonium inevitable in the early stages of a popular insurrection and given, too, the military campaign and the freewheeling, hectic, headlong pace of change, where events continually outran their originators, the United Irishmen created a minor miracle in Wexford town, coolly running an "embryo Republick" (Musgrave) for three weeks during the turbulent height of the Rebellion itself. In many ways, this Republic was the closest parallel which Ireland had to offer to the experience of the French Revolution, marked as it was by the assumption of power by a new leadership, with popular support and a Republican ideology. How did this Wexford Republic come about?

Wexford town in the 1790s was a real hotbed of political mobilisation and debate. A prosperous county town with a population of around 10,000, it had grown wealthy on malt and maintained a fleet of 100 ships engaged in shipping it to Dublin. Because it was an 'open' borough, it was politically free and not under the whim of a local magnate, as were New Ross (Tottenham), Gorey (Ram), Enniscorthy (Colclough), or Fethard (Loftus). Its Protestant burgesses and freemen could vote in elections and the town was split politically between those who favoured reform (liberals) and those who wished to see the *status quo* maintained (conservatives). In particular, the issue of repeal of the penal laws against Catholics split the town's 3,000 Protestants down the middle.

The liberal, pro-Catholic emancipation faction of the town was led by the Harvey, Grogan and Colclough families with support from the Hattons, Letts and Keugh, among others. The conservative 'Protestant Ascendancy' stance was supported by George Ogle and the Marquis of Ely, with support from the Boyds.

Another important element in the political ferment in the town was the reactivated Catholics, who were fighting hard to regain participation in municipal and national politics, denied them by the Penal Laws. Wealthy, educated, outward-looking, impatient, these men were prominent in the public life not just of Wexford but of Dublin, where they were very active in the national Catholic Committee. Their key leaders were James Edward Devereux and

Edward Hay, with assistance from William Kearney, Robert Meyler and Edward Sutton.

When the United Irishmen became active in Wexford town in 1797 and 1798, their adherents included a formidable alliance of liberal Protestants (Bagenal Harvey, Matthew Keugh, Cornelius Grogan, William Hatton) and Catholic activists (Hay, Robert Carthy, William Kearney), who formed a potent non-sectarian alliance. This alliance, the first to break the sectarian mould of 18th century Irish politics, alarmed the reactionary 'Dublin Castle' men in the county who favoured the 'not an inch' approach to governing Ireland. Their bitter language, harsh security measures and biased law created recruits for the United Irishmen in the spring of 1798. Many of the leading United men shared another common thread - close ties to France: men such as Edward Sweetman, John and Edward Hay, William Kearney, William Barker, Edward Sutton, James Edward Devereux. Thus, when the rebellion finally erupted, these men were not alone its natural leaders, they were also well schooled in the lessons of Revolutionary France.

Once Wexford town fell into their hands, they immediately set up a provisional Government of the newly proclaimed Wexford Republic, putting into practice the ideas which before had only floated around pub, inn, coffee house and tavern. A small executive Directory was formed, composed of that distinctive United Irishman merger of Protestant reformers and Catholic activists, who had led the 'alternative' political culture of Wexford town in the 1790s.

Matthew Keugh (also the Military Governor), Bagenal Harvey (with his secretary, Nicholas Grey) and William Hatton joined forces with Edward Hay, Robert Meyler, Robert Carthy and William Kearney to form the seven-man Directory, which met in the sympathetic environment of the liberal gentry's town houses: the Letts, Colcloughs and Harveys. A more popular 'Senate' of 500 met at the 'Senate House' of Wexford - the most elaborate business premises of the town, Cullimores of Main Street. This second tier of control - the middle management - was made up essentially of the Catholic merchants and shopkeepers of the town, especially those radicalised in the 1790s. They were part of the generation schooled in the lessons of the American and French revolutions, more especially 'The Rights of Man'. These men would have been highly conscious of their exclusion from the monolithically protestant corporation - the 'Wexford

Republick' offered these propertied men their first taste of democratic rights. They included Edward Frayne (tanner), John Herron (chandler), John Murphy (shopkeeper), Patrick Prendergast (maltster), John Scallan (shipowner) and John Howlin (ex-American privateer and shipowner). The very real achievement of the 'Directory' and the 'Senate' was to maintain order and discipline in the town over the three weeks of the Republic.

Even so obnoxious a personage as Lord Kingsborough, leader of the hated North Cork Militia was safely jailed during it. The peace was maintained by involving the whole town in a series of democratically elected committees, who looked after various aspects of administration, such as rationing and patrolling.

Each area looked after its own needs - especially the suburbs, with their strong sense of stalwart independence and occupational solidarity. Thus, John Street (home of the butchers and tanners), the Faythe (fishermen and sailors) and Selskar (merchants and shopkeepers) all had their own committees, their own fighting corps and their own elected leader - like Dick Monk, the ex-shoeblack and 'Mayor of John Street', who was captain of the 300-strong John Street corps.

Other efficient arrangements were made: the Bull Ring was turned into an open air munitions factory and experiments (conducted by Edward Hay) were made on gunpowder manufacture. Stirring proclamations (as well as more mundane rationing coupons) were printed at Christopher Taylor's printshop, whose new-found status as 'Printer to the Wexford Republick' was emblazoned in gold letters on his door. A rebel navy, under John Scallan and John Howlin, was assembled. Passwords, strict patrols, orchestrated parades and morning manoeuvres on the quay were the order of the day, introduced by the impressive Matthew Keugh to maintain military and civil discipline.

The Directory stage-managed two exemplary executions of informers to illustrate their control and there was a functioning 'committee of public safety'. The executions were handled as public displays of order, with a massive parade, muffled drums beating out the Dead March, and all the pomp of military ritual. Popular participation in the 'Republick' was signalled in the green boughs which profusely decorated every home, and the words, 'Liberty' and

'Equality' which were painted on many doors. Trees of Liberty were also planted, around which the people danced, shouting *'Vive la République'* and *'Éireann go brách'* in a striking echo of the French Revolution.

The astonishing degree of control experienced during the Wexford Republic is illustrated by the macabre *dénouement* when the organisation collapsed under the weight of impending military defeat - the massacre of 93 innocent prisoners on Wexford bridge. The rebel army is frequently depicted by hostile commentators as a drunken, infuriated, ungovernable mob, a chaotic mass of ignorant peasants. Similarly, the rebellion in Wexford is reduced to a sectarian or agrarian phenomenon. The hidden history of the Wexford Republic reveals the simplistic sterility of such views. It offers a fascinating glimpse of the non-military side of the United Irishmen - and a tantalising peek into the possible future if the United Irishmen had staged a successful *coup* in 1798.●

Lord Edward Fitzgerald

73

NEW FROM CORK UNIVERSITY PRESS

FELLOWSHIP OF FREEDOM: THE UNITED IRISHMEN AND THE 1798 REBELLION
Kevin Whelan

CORK
UNIVERSITY
PRESS

Published in association with the major 1798 Exhibition this richly illustrated and timely book is essential reading for anyone seeking an insight into this remarkable period in Irish history.
ISBN 1 85918 209 7 £25.00 Hb
ISBN 1 85918 210 0 £14.95 Pb
full colour, illustrated throughout, 200pp
May

VERSE IN ENGLISH FROM EIGHTEENTH-CENTURY IRELAND
editor, *Andrew Carpenter*

The poems in this pioneering anthology introduce many previously neglected writers to a general readership, and give a fresh and vivid insight into almost every aspect of life in eighteenth-century Ireland.

ISBN 1 85918 103 1 £40.00 Hb
ISBN 1 85918 104 X £15.95 Pb, 640pp
February

**ANDREW BRYSON'S ORDEAL:
AN EPILOGUE TO THE 1798 REBELLION**
IRISH NARRATIVES SERIES
editor, *Michael Durey*

Andrew Bryson was punished for his part in the 1798 rebellion by compulsory enlistment in the regular army. A long and reflective letter provides a vivid chronicle of his enforced travels through Ireland and beyond. The first title in a major new series, offering readers interested in Irish history a unique opportunity to discover fresh primary sources in the form of personal testimony.

ISBN: 1 85918 144 9 £8.95 Pb, 128pp
March

For further information please contact:
Cork University Press, Crawford Business Park, Crosses Green, Cork, Ireland
Tel: 021 902980, Fax: 021 315329, e-mail: corkunip@ucc.ie
Visit our website: www.ucc.ie/corkunip

The United Scotsmen and the Events of 1798

by Peter Berresford Ellis

In January, 1798, the London government's agents there uncovered plans for a general uprising in Scotland and the establishment of a Scottish republic. Scottish republicans were in close contact with the United Irishmen. Nine prominent Scotsmen, including progressive members of the London parliament and several Scottish peers, were named as members of the 'Provisional Government of the Scottish Republic'. The president of this government was a young Scottish lawyer named Thomas Muir. Muir had already been sentenced to fourteen years transportation to the penal colony at Botany Bay but had made a daring escape in an American warship and made his way to France where he had been honoured as the first non-Frenchman to be made a citizen of the republic.

Peter Berresford Ellis is a historian and author. Among his works are
A History of the Irish Working Class (1972) and *The Rising of the Moon* (1987).

The Scottish republican movement had started its life about the same time as the Irish movement in the aftermath of the American War of Independence and the French Revolution. A movement called The Friends of the People had been formed to sever the Union of 1707 and establish an independent Scottish republic. The president of its convention in 1793, Basil William Hamilton, Lord Daer, declared:

> Scotland has long groaned under the chains of England and knows its connections there have been the cause of its greatest misfortunes ... we have been the worse of every connection with you. The Friends of Liberty in Scotland have almost universally been enemies to the Union with England.

Thomas Muir had been a prominent leader of this movement and during trips to Belfast, where he was a friend of Napper Tandy, he had been made an honorary member of the United Irishmen. He even opened links with another Celtic country, Brittany, where he was in touch with the Marquis La Fayette, who had fought in the American War of Independence, with hundreds of Bretons. It was from Brittany that the French Revolution had actually been given its kick-start.

La Fayette had made an impassioned plea for continuing the Breton parliament when the French decided to abolish it. Armand Kersaint, another Breton republican, made an interesting address to the French National Assembly, reported in *Le Moniteur*, January 3rd, 1790:

> The English people, like all conquerors, have long oppressed Scotland and Ireland; but it should be noted that these two nations, always restive, and secretly in revolt against the injustices of the dominating race, have acquired at different epochs concessions which have engendered the hope of ultimately regaining their entire independence... Since the Union, Scotland has been represented in Parliament, but out of such proportion to its wealth, its extent and its population, that it does not conceal the fact that it is nothing but a dependent colony of the English Government.
>
> Yet the Scots know their rights and their strength; the principles developed by the French nation have found zealous defenders who have been the first to merit the honour of being persecuted by the British Government; but these persecutions have made proselytes, and nowhere is more joy caused by your victories than in Scotland, the principal towns of which have been illuminated to honour them ...

In July, 1793, Muir was arrested returning from Paris via Ireland. He had able defenders, including the Irish playwright Richard Brinsley Sheridan and the Earl of Stair and Earl of Stanhope. Indeed, Muir had popular international connections. American President George Washington personally ordered the United States warship, *The Oner*, commanded by Captain Dawes, to rescue Muir from the penal colony in New South Wales. Washington even offered Muir a position in the United States. Muir declined.

Having successfully reached Paris after managing amazing adventures, including being badly wounded in a brush with an English warship in Cadiz Bay, he arrived in Paris and was given a house in Chantilly which became the intellectual centre of the Scottish republicans. Indeed, many Irish revolutionaries, like Napper Tandy, were visitors.

Many leaders of the Friends of the People had, however, been arrested and tried for crimes from high treason to sedition. Robert Watt and David Downie had been arrested with incriminating plans for an uprising in which Edinburgh Castle was to be seized. Robert Watt became the first Scottish republican to suffer the death sentence. After being hanged, his head was cut off and thrown to the people.

The last of several leaders of the Friends of the People to be sentenced to fourteen years transportation in 1794, Joseph Gerrald, had told the court that the English had deprived the Scottish people of their rights from the time of the Union of 1707. "But if that Union has operated to rob us of our rights, it is our objective to regain them!"

With most of the leadership of the Friends of the People arrested, a new totally secret revolutionary organisation had to be organised. It was called the United Scotsmen, taking its name from the Irish model. By the Spring of 1797, the United Scotsmen were active, based on local cells of not more than sixteen people sending a delegate to committees at parochial, then county and then national level. The National Convention met every seven weeks, usually within the vicinity of Glasgow, Stirling or Edinburgh.

There was a seven man executive which governed the movement. Lord Daer, whom the authorities had not touched because of his family connections, was a member. Lord Hugh Sempill of Beltrees (Renfrew), was another. William Maitland, Earl of Lauderdale, Colonel Norman MacLeod, a Whig Member of Parliament for

Inverness, the Earl of Buchan and Sinclair Campbell of Glenorchy also served on the executive. Robert Fergusson was another member and he was said to be the grandson of the Robert Ferguson of Aberdeen who had been involved in the Presbyterian plot to assassinate William of Orange. Another member was Sorley Bell (referred to in English reports as 'Sorbelloni'). Angus Cameron, a tradesman from Weem, Perth, was also a member.

In 1797 affairs came to a head in Scotland mainly due to the Militia Act in which the government had passed a law conscripting able bodied Scots males, between nineteen and twenty-three years old, for military service. Riots were breaking out in Kirkintilloch, Freuchie, Strathaven, Galston, Dalry and throughout Aberdeen. The Government responded by sending in troops. People were being killed and wounded. .In January, 1797, the French had mistakenly sent troops to England. The plan was to land two armies, one at Bristol and one at Hull, appealing to English republicans to join them. The armies were commanded by American and Irish officers. By mistake the troops heading for Bristol landed at Fishguard. It was a silly mistake. The situation in England was different than in Ireland and Scotland and the English with republican sympathies were English first and republican afterwards. The French had also tried to land in Bantry Bay in December, 1796, and this caused General Lake to start disarming the United Irishmen in Ulster.

Whether there was a disagreement among the National Executive as to the time to strike is not clear. But, it appears, Angus Cameron of Perth decided to act on his own and issued a call to the United Scotsmen to rise in Perth. His second-in-command was James Menzies Junior, a Weem merchant whose brother was the famous botanist Archibald Menzies of Weem (1754-1841) who had fought in the American War of Independence. Reports indicate that 16,000 men answered Cameron's call. They included a cavalry regiment.

The United Scotsmen had initial success. They captured Castle Menzies and they forced Sir John Menzies to declare against the Militia Act. They marched on Blair Castle where the Duke of Atholl was forced to surrender. Then a detachment went to Taymouth Castle, near Kenmore, residence of the Earls of Breadalbane. This was also a military headquarters and the United Scotsmen were able to seize its armoury.

Thousands of English troops poured into the country. These line regiments were used because the commander in Scotland was afraid of sending Scottish troops against their fellow countrymen. Faced with superior forces, Cameron proved a good commander. His army simply melted back into the population. He and Menzies were never caught and eventually settled in America. On July 17th, 1797, an Act of Parliament declared the United Scotsmen illegal and any member liable to an immediate seven years transportation. In November, 1797, trials for sedition started and George Mealmaker, a Dundee weaver, was sentenced to fourteen years, while other members received various terms of transportation and imprisonment. Two prominent organisers, Archibald Gray and a man named Dyer, were able to escape from prison and make their way to Hamburg in Germany.

The exact aims of the rising were discovered in papers found by government agents in January, 1798. A special House of Commons Committee was sent up to investigate matters.

Over the next four years, many Scotsmen were to be tried for treason and sedition as members of the United Scotsmen. Men like Robert Jaffrey, David Black and James Paterson in September, 1798, who, from the dock, applauded the United Irishmen's uprising. There was a former militia sergeant William Maxwell, who was tried on June 23rd 1800 and given seven years transportation having been found to be an organiser and circulator of United Scotsmen propaganda.

The last record of a United Scotsman having been tried before the courts for the serious crime of sedition was the trial in 1802 of Thomas Wilson, a Fife weaver, and a delegate to the National Convention.

There were many other trials on less serious charges. The most tragic blow to the United Scotsmen was, of course, the death in January, 1799, at the age of thirty-three of Thomas Muir at Chantilly. His death was caused by the wounds received in the fight with the English man o'war.

Among veterans of the Friends of the People and the United Scotsmen was James Wilson of Strathaven. He had become active in 1792. A literate man, he was a weaver by profession and a delegate to the National Convention. In 1820, aged 63, then a grandfather, Wilson, true to his principles, took up his gun and joined the younger men in answering the call in the 1820 insurrection in Scotland. In the aftermath of that insurrection he was one of 85 prisoners to be charged with High Treason. He was hanged and then beheaded. His last words on the scaffold were: "I die a true patriot for the cause of freedom for my poor country". This year we will see many 1798 commemorations. In Scotland, the 1820 is annually commemorated at the graves where its executed leaders lay buried (in Sighthill and in Strathaven).

As Scotland begins its tentative steps towards finally achieving its own parliament, one is aware of asense of excitement and change in the air ... changes in the status for all the nations on these islands. Perhaps the sacrifice and aspirations of the United Scotsmen will now be accorded a proper place in history. ●

Thomas Muir,
United Scotsman

United In Our Common Interest
Ideas More Pertinent Than Ever

by Jim McVeigh

Almost two hundred years ago one of the most violent and tragic events in Ireland's history occurred: the rebellion of 1798. According to Thomas Pakenham

> In the space of a few short weeks, 30,000 people - peasants armed with pikes and pitch forks, defenceless women and children - were cut down or shot or blown like chaff as they charged up the mouth of the cannon. (*The Year of Liberty, The History of the Great Irish Rebellion of 1798*, Phoenix):

Jim McVeigh is a member of Sinn Féin. He is currently a prisoner in the H Blocks.

By the end of the rebellion the bulk of its leaders were either dead or in prison. The fragile unity of Catholic, Protestant and Dissenter, so carefully fostered by the men and women of the United Irish movement, was shattered. Many of those Presbyterians who had so eagerly received the revolutionary ideas of Republicanism now deserted the cause, and in just a few short years the Act of Union would secure the connection with Britain that Tone so desired to break.

It would be fair to say that by almost any standard the rebellion was a failure. Why then should so distant an event be worthy of our interest? What relevance could it possibly have to the problems and concerns of the Irish people today?

When we examine the men and women of 1798 and their stories, we are moved by their acts of great courage and sacrifice. But these qualities alone do little to explain their enduring legacy. The rebellion and the politics of its adversaries remain relevant today because the fundamental problems that ignited the struggle also remain with us. Our country remains deeply divided, geographically and along class and sectarian lines. Part of the country is occupied by a foreign power and our sovereignty denied us. In such circumstances it is hardly surprising that the political programme of the United Irish movement should have such resonance, particularly for northern nationalists:

> To subvert the tyranny of our execrable government, to break the connection with England, the never failing source of all our political evils, and to assert the independence of my country, these were my objects ... To unite the whole people of Ireland, to abolish the memory of all past dissensions, and to substitute the common name of Irishman in place of the denominations of Protestant, Catholic and Dissenter - these were my means. (Wolfe Tone)

In Ireland the agrarian unrest of the 18th century has been replaced by industrial unrest and working class alienation. In the north religious discrimination is still widespread practice, sectarian murder commonplace. In a recent court case (*The Irish Times*, March 3rd, 1998) the southern state's failure to provide accommodation for vulnerable children was remarked upon by a High Court judge, individuals not usually noted for their radicalism, when he said the "much vaunted Celtic tiger" was not looking after its young. In the same issue of

The Irish Times another piece, entitled "Racist slogans painted on walls in Ennis", highlighted the growing problem of racism in Irish society. The problem of drug abuse is endemic in parts of our cities, and spreading, poverty remains entrenched as the gap between rich and poor widens, north and south. Women, travellers, gays and handicapped people continue to be excluded within society.

In 1791 Wolfe Tone penned *An Argument on Behalf of the Catholics of Ireland.* It would be difficult to find a more eloquent or more stinging attack upon sectarianism or the politics of exclusion. Both he and his comrades had no time for the hypocrisy of those men and women who turned a blind eye to the injustices of his day and yet spoke of freedom and justice:

> We prate and babble, and write books, and publish them, filled with sentiments of freedom, and abhorrence of tyranny, and lofty praises of the Rights of man! Yet we are content to hold three millions of our fellow creatures and fellow subjects, in degradation and infamy and contempt, or, to sum up all in one word, in slavery!

Too many of our politicians, Church, business and trade union leaders, the comfortable classes, are only too willing to ignore the injustices of today or to pay passing lip service to them. The vested interests of his time refused to support the United Irish rebellion because, in Tone's words, "they trembled for their titles and estates".

How little some things have changed. Of course the world and Ireland have changed. Industrialisation and global capitalisation has enriched a relatively small group of nations and we are now fortunate to be among them. But the rest of the world, the greater portion of its population, continues to experience abject poverty, hunger, famine and war. While the gap between rich and poor within Ireland widens, so too has the gap between rich and poor nations.

The political creed of the United Irish movement was not a narrow xenophobic one, not at all. They drew their inspiration from revolutionary France and America and could see beyond Ireland's problems to the world around them. This spirit of solidarity and internationalism, a spirit so relevant in the world today, developed because, according to Wolfe Tone, "as we knew experimentally what it was to be enslaved, we sympathised most sincerely with the French people, and watched their progress to freedom with the utmost anxiety

Today along the Falls Road in Belfast, or on the streets and walls of Derry, images of Nelson Mandela, Che Guevara, ETA or the PLO are as common as the names of Wolfe Tone or Bobby Sands. Having endured oppression we continue to watch the progress of freedom throughout the world.

"If men could only learn from history, what lessons it might teach us", wrote Samuel Coleridge Taylor. Over the 200 years since the Rebellion of 1798 Ireland has repeatedly revisited the same battles. In 1922 part of the island achieved a measure of self-government following a war of independence and a brutal civil conflict. A few decades later years of simmering anger and resentment exploded in the north and the current conflict began. Partition has failed and every attempt to reform the state has satisfied no one, either Unionist or Nationalist. Even in the Ireland of today the ideals of 'Liberty, Equality and Fraternity' adopted by the United Irish movement seem to be more pertinent than ever. For Irish Catholic, Protestant and Dissenter, and indeed those of no creed at all, the two hundredth anniversary of the Rebellion presents us with an opportunity to rediscover a rich political philosophy and a moment in our history when we were, for a period, united in our common interest.

> Let them but consider what union has done in small states, what discord in great ones. Let them look to their government, let them look to their fellow slaves, who, by coalition with them, may rise to be their fellow citizens, and form a new order in their society, a new era in their history (Theobald Wolfe Tone) ●

The Rising of 1798

by Seán O'Brádaigh

The Rising of 1798 was Separatist, Republican and Democratic in its objectives. Ever since the Anglo-Norman invasion of 1169 Irish Separatists resisted England's claim to occupy and rule Ireland. The native Irish, for example the O'Neills and O'Donnells and those of Norman stock who became Irish, like the FitzGeralds and Patrick Sarsfield, endeavoured to win back Irish independence.

Seán Ó Brádaigh is a member of Republican Sinn Féin, and is Cathaoirleach, Coiste Cuimhneacháin Náisiúnta (1798 Commemoration Committee)

The century which followed the Treaty of Limerick (1691) was one of the most wretched in Irish history. In 1727 Dean Swift commented that:

The dress and appearance of the people is miserable – the families of farmers who pay great rents are living on potatoes and buttermilk, without a shoe or stocking to their feet.

The land had been seized in the various Plantations over the centuries and the peasantry paid rents to landlords (often absent) who charged what rents they pleased, and which were collected through middlemen. The Church of Ireland was the established church and Catholics were deprived of their rights under the Penal laws; Presbyterians suffered disabilities but to a lesser extent. In 1740 over 400,000 people died of starvation.

Societies like the Whiteboys were organised to fight back against the injustice of the system. The Irish people yearned for their ancient rights and their freedom. Most of them spoke Irish and many of their songs praised Bonnie Prince Charlie and the Scottish Stuarts, whom they regarded as allies against English tyranny.

But a new dawn was awakening. In Europe it was the Age of Enlightenment and Reason, with talk of ending Monarchy and establishing Democracy. France gave the lead when the fall of the Bastille heralded the Revolution in 1789. *'Liberty, Equality, Fraternity'* became the rallying cry of the Revolutionaries.

In the New World the American colonists fought and won their own War of Independence (1776-1781) against England. Monarchs trembled on their thrones as their 'Divine Right' was questioned, the Rights of Man were debated and the new Republics of France and the United States were established.

Theobald Wolfe Tone, a law graduate of Trinity College, Dublin and a Protestant, along with others, mostly Presbyterians, founded the Society of United Irishmen in Belfast in October 1791. A Dublin Society was founded three weeks later and a newspaper called the *Northern Star* was launched. Their initial demands were for reform, "a society of equality which would include people of all religious persuasions – and of none". Tone had previously worked strenuously and effectively for the rights of Catholics, but the British government of the time opposed the moderate demands of the United Irishmen. They refused to concede Equality, Democracy and Civil Rights. Gradually the United movement became more Radical and Republican.

After 1793 England was at war with France and she chose the path of coercion in Ireland, using strong-arm tactics against the reformers. They brought in an Insurrection Act in 1796 and Martial Law was imposed in many areas in 1797. The United Irishmen sought the help of the new French Republic and prepared to fight for an Irish Republic. "Break the connection with England," declared Tone.

In December 1796 a French fleet of 46 ships carrying an army of 14,000 men sailed from the port of Brest under the command of General Lazare Hoche. Wolfe Tone accompanied them and they planned to land at Bantry Bay, seize the city of Cork and then with a general uprising they would march on Dublin, the centre of English rule. Winter storms scattered the fleet, only 16 vessels reached Bantry and even then the weather made a landing impossible. They sailed back to France. More French expeditions were planned and the United Irishmen hesitated between striking first or waiting until the French would actually arrive. Meanwhile the Government of England brought in more emergency laws and the Yeomanry (mostly Protestant) and Militias (mostly Catholic) as well as the regular English regiments were used to terrorise the populace. Pitch caps, floggings and half-hangings were used to extract information from people. Informers were paid huge sums to betray their comrades.

The Rising itself was planned for May 23, 1798. In the event, the main centres of Irish resistance to English rule were in Wexford, Antrim and Down. But there was action in other areas also, including Wicklow, Carlow, Kilkenny, Kildare, Meath, Dublin, Westmeath, Longford, Cork, Tipperary and in the West later in the year.

The Wexford Insurgents drove the Crown Forces out of County Wexford and attempted to spread the rising to Counties Carlow, Kilkenny and Wicklow, with Dublin city as their major objective. Armed mostly with pikes they fought with great skill and determination. As most of the country failed to rise simultaneously the English brought massive forces to bear on the Wexfordmen at New Ross, Arklow and eventually at Vinegar Hill near Enniscorthy where the Wexford Rising was effectively crushed on June 21, 1798.

The people of Wexford are justly proud of their achievement, their bravery and example in 1798. The names of leaders like Father Murphy and Bagenal Harvey are remembered with pride and the Wexford pike and pikemen are symbols of their heroic contribution to the fight for Irish freedom.

In Antrim and Down the Dissenters or Presbyterians were prominent in the Rising, and the insurgents occupied several towns in both counties, showing great valour against a formidable enemy. Henry Joy McCracken led the attack on Antrim town on June 7 and was afterwards court-martialled and hanged in the Cornmarket in Belfast. In County Down Henry Munro led the insurgents to victory at Saintfield, but they also were defeated at Ballynahinch on June 13. He was hanged in front of his home in Lisburn. Historians record that 30 Presbyterian ministers were involved in the Rising and several of them were hanged by the Crown.

General Lake, Commander of British Forces in Ireland, earned the name of the 'Butcher of Wexford' because of the severity of the measures he used to suppress the Rising.

When news of the Rising reached France the Republican Government ordered the organisation of three expeditions, under Generals Humbert, Hardy and Kilmaine to sail to Ireland "to help the United Irish who have taken up arms to throw off the yoke of English oppression". General Jean-Joseph Humbert's small army of 1,100 men landed in Killala, County Mayo in August. They were joined by the 'Men of the West' and together they won a spectacular victory at Castlebar on August 27th. Humbert liberated Mayo, proclaimed a Republic of Connacht and marched audaciously across five counties, penetrating as far as County Longford where he was eventually forced to surrender at Ballinamuck on September 8.

General Hardy's army of 3,000 men reached Loch Swilly, County Donegal, on October 12th. Their fleet of 10 ships was intercepted and defeated by the Royal Navy and Wolfe Tone was arrested and brought to Dublin in chains. He told his captors: "For the cause which I have embraced, I feel prouder to wear these chains, than if I were decorated with the Star and Garter of England". He was tried by court-martial and sentenced to death. He died in prison in suspicious circumstances after the Chief Justice had issued a writ to suspend his execution. He was aged 35.

The man who organised his generation to bring about an Ireland united, independent and democratic was buried in Bodenstown, County Kildare.

Two hundred years later his aims have not yet been achieved. This is indeed a sobering thought.

God grant you glory, brave Father Murphy
And open Heaven to all your men;
For the cause that called you may call tomorrow
In another fight for the Green again.
(PJ McCall)

It is estimated that 30,000 people died in the Rising of 1798. To those gallant people who suffered and sacrificed so much we owe an enormous debt of gratitude. Under the United Irish leadership Irish separatism became one of the most progressive movements in the world, seeking as well as national independence, Equality, Democracy and the Rights of Man. Irish women made their own important contribution and the names of Molly Doyle of Wexford, Anne Devlin of Wicklow and Betsy Gray of Down are remembered too for their courage and fidelity to the cause.

Robert Emmet (1803), the Young Irelanders (1848), the Fenians (1867) and the Irish Volunteers and Irish Citizen Army (1916) were all in the same Republican Separatist tradition of the United Irishmen. In more recent times, Bobby Sands, Republican MP for Fermanagh and South Tyrone, and his comrades who died on hunger strike in Long Kesh Camp and in English prisons, represent the ultimate sacrifice in Ireland's long struggle for freedom. The true Republicans of today are those who actively strive to end English rule in Ireland and establish the sovereignty, democracy and rights of the Irish Nation.

Patrick Pearse was clear and eloquent in his interpretation of Irish Republican objectives. There was no evasion, equivocation or double-talk when he wrote, at Christmas, 1915:

If we today are fighting for something either greater than or less than the thing our fathers fought for, either our fathers did not fight for freedom at all, or we are not fighting for freedom. If I do not hold the faith of Tone, and if Tone was not a heretic, then I am.

If Tone said 'BREAK the connection with England', and if I say 'MAINTAIN the connection with England', I may be preaching a saner (as I am certainly preaching a safer) gospel than his, but I am obviously not preaching the same gospel.

Separatism, in fact, is the national position. Whenever an Irish leader has taken up a position different from the national position he has been repudiated by the next generation. The United Irishmen repudiated Grattan. The Young Irelanders repudiated Daniel O'Connell. The Irish Volunteers have repudiated Mr Redmond. The chain of the Separatist tradition has never once snapped during the centuries.

The Irish Republican Movement was founded 200 years ago. Despite English might, native collaboration and misrepresentation this Movement has endured to this day, in its aims and methods, to break the connection with England and establish national and civil rights in Ireland. This continuity is the guarantee of ultimate success.

To break the connection with England, the never-failing source of all our political evils, and to assert the independence of my country – these were my objects. To unite the whole people of Ireland, to abolish the memory of all past dissensions, and to substitute the common name of Irishman in place of the denominations of Protestant, Catholic and Dissenter – these were my means.

From my earliest youth I have regarded the connection between Ireland and Great Britain as the curse of the Irish nation, and felt convinced that, whilst it lasted, this country could never be free nor happy.

Ómós An Phiarsaigh

Dob é Tiobóid Wolfe Tone an fear dob fhearr de Ghaeil ná de Ghall-Ghaeil dar gineadh riamh in Éirinn. Cromaimid ár gceann agus feacaimid ár nglún ina fhianaise, agus gairimid é thar ar síolraíodh de dhea-fhearaibh anseo ó dealbhadh Éire, ar mhórgacht a anama, ar dhoimhneacht a intleachta, ar mhéid a fhóirithine do chlanna Gael. Ní bheadh Éire ann inniu mura mbeadh an fear sin. A chuimhne sin agus a theagasc sin do choinnigh beo go nuige seo í.

Dob uafar í doimhneacht intleachta Wolfe Tone agus dob iontach í géire a intinne. Do thuig sé dála Gael agus cúrsaí Gall go hiomlán. Dob é an chéad duine do thuig ina gceart iad. Is é a thug léargas agus solas ar an gcúis sin dá dtáinig ina dhiaidh.

An Piarsach, 1912 ●

200 years since 1798, 150 years since the Communist Manifesto

Ireland and Marxism in the Nineteenth Century

The Political Link Between Irish Republicanism, Chartism and Early Marxism

by Harry Vince

The human link between 1798 republicanism and the international workers' movement which Marx and Engels wanted to build, especially its British component into which Marx and Engels inserted themselves 50 years after 1798, is to be found through the Industrial Revolution and the part played by emigrant Irish people in it.

Harry Vince is an artist, he became an active socialist in London in 1963.
He has been a member of both the Irish and British Labour Parties.

91

Wave after wave of Irish people emigrated to the industrial centres of England from 1800, above all in the early period, to Lancashire, Manchester and the towns of the North. British industrial production grew by 22.9% from 1800-1810, by 38.6% from 1810-1820 and by 47.2% from 1820-30. One of the main engines for this was cotton production, and one of the main sources of labour in Liverpool and the cotton towns of Lancashire was Irish immigrants. According to Eric Hobsbawm (*Industry and Empire*, Penguin, 1972)

> they came as members of a pauperized, degraded peasantry whose own native society had been crushed by some centuries of English oppression into fragments of old custom, mutual aid and kinship solidarity ...

Exactly 50 years after the United Irish revolution of 1798 was rising to its bitter climax and during the period of massive growth of the Irish industrial proletariat in England Karl Marx wrote the first draft of the *Communist Manifesto*. He would have heard of the revolutionary tradition in Ireland from his friend Friedrich Engels.

In February 1848, he went to Paris to take part in the revolution there, and thence to Germany for the same reason. Marx and Engels strove to push the boundaries of the revolutions of 1848, from what they saw as petty bourgeois democracy, to those of 'proletarian revolution'.

The national question arose, in various forms, in many of the countries where the revolutions of 1848 occurred, and Marx had to deal with it. At that time the thinking of Marx and Engels on the role of nations was undergoing rapid transition. The *Communist Manifesto* stated that:

> National differences, and antagonisms between peoples, are daily more and more vanishing, owing to the development of the bourgeoisie, to freedom of commerce, to the world market ...

It also says, *a propos* the working class, that it has

> no country. We cannot take from them what they have not got. Since the proletariat must first of all acquire political supremacy, must rise to be the leading class of the nation, must constitute itself as the nation, it is, so far, itself national, though not in the bourgeois sense of the word.

These might be called the principled or abstracted positions on which Marx and Engels stood. Their handling of the national question varied in practice. In 1848 they believed in tactical alliances with revolutionary nationalists, although they had not begun to work out the differences between the nationalism of oppressed nations and the chauvinism of great nations. The *Communist Manifesto* supported the Polish "party that insists on an agrarian revolution as the prime condition for national emancipation..." Marx believed that some nations, including the Poles, had forged the right to self-determination through generations of struggle. Others, such as the Czechs, he was doubtful about, even if they were oppressed. As late as 1895 Engels was writing (in the Introduction to *The Class Struggles in France*, Karl Marx) that by 1866

> the independence and internal unity of the great nations, with the exception of Poland, had become a fact. Within relatively modest limits, it is true, but, for all that, on a scale large enough to allow the development of the working class to proceed without finding national complications any longer a serious issue.

This was said in a Europe which contained Czechs, Slovaks, Hungarians, Croats, Slovenes, Ruthenes and Poles within the Austrian Empire, numberless oppressed peoples within the Russian Tsarate and Ireland within the United Kingdom. We should not forget Algeria, destined to be part of France ... Later in the same volume Marx wrote, as a kind of truism, "The irony of world history turns everything upside down." The national question was destined to do this to the Marxist dogma of abstract 'internationalism', if not to the core values of Marxism. Engels had written, 36 years earlier, that "logical exposition need by no means be confined to the purely abstract sphere. On the contrary, it requires historical illustration and continuous contact with reality." Marxists, in relation to the national question, would seem to have proceeded from abstraction, rather than contact with reality, with some honourable exceptions.

The fact that the younger Marx felt able to link the agrarian problem in Poland so directly with national liberation could have opened a door onto a series of problems through which the independence of nation states can be linked to the development of productive forces within and between them. The development of agriculture into a more modern, productive form, the building of an industrial infrastructure and the removal of feudal remnants from power were not elements original to Marx. His generation had inherited but modified them from the thinking of the Enlightenment, especially the French and Scottish economists. Marx viewed national economic development as providing the material through which a proletariat could emerge to play its given role in a new international revolutionary process. National political independence was not an end in itself.

Yet both Marx and Engels were well capable of grasping that there could be other, cultural and historical, processes at work, which well preceded the Enlightenment. The young Engels was prone to write poetry, one of which sees the relationship between the Seminole Indians in Florida and the white coloniser, from both sides, with an introduction by "The Spirit of Earth". Engels could be accused of romanticising the 'noble savage' when he wrote, as the voice of The Seminole:

So would the White men hunt you ruthlessly.
But let your speeding arrows make it clear
That they're the quarry, and the hunters - we.
They envy us our red skins; and in fear
That their revolting white may be discerned,
They swathe themselves in many coloured gear.

The White Man responds:

In seven years of expiation
I've fully paid my debt in iron bonds.
In a swift ship they bring me o'er the sea
To Liberty - but on an alien strand ....
For me, new Freedom, so I hoped, begins.
But Freedom fighters seek my murder here.

There truly were not many men who could write about such things this way in 1839. Later Engels was to subsume the individual and the cultural into a broader vision of history, that of Marx, but his was a humane and lyrical socialism.

Marx had a more abstract and historicist cast of mind. The creation of strong capitalist nations in Europe was the context in which Marx viewed these problems at the time. This was the period of rampant capitalist expansion, the acquisition of colonies and the pre-dawn of imperialist capital proper. But Marx was far from being an exponent of history as an external machine. He wrote that

> History does nothing; it 'possesses no colossal riches'; it 'fights no fight.' It is rather man - real, living man - who acts, possesses and fights in everything. It is by no means 'History' which uses man as a means to carry out its ends as if it were a person apart; rather History is nothing but the activity of man in pursuit of his ends. (*The Holy Family*)

This remains one of the strongest criticisms that can be made of the vacation of responsibility for and in history by the post-modernists.

Ireland was in an almost unique position, having been held as a feudal dominion and then quasi-integrated colony in Europe for hundreds of years already, a process which had profoundly affected economic relations within the country, and virtually stifled its cultural, political and economic maturation at the same time as trying to mediate its international relations through England, its language and its economy. The American colonies, perhaps the nearest equivalent, had a somewhat different internal experience. They had to create anew the economic, political and cultural foundations of a nation, while completely and almost universally displacing an indigenous population which had been involved, as allies, in wars between the different colonisers, Britain and France, but was excluded, along with the African slaves, as a component of the revolutionary nation in formation. No part of the Irish nation was excluded in this way by the revolutionary nationalism of the 1790s. But the Enlightenment concept of nationhood did not extend outside Europe. In a sense the new American nation had to be understood as a kind of exceptional, displaced or extended, part of Europe, with a European population and culture.

The Haitian slaves clearly were ready to forge a nation and had the ideology and organisational structures to do so, but not so far as Napoleon was concerned. Native American Indians, who were pushed to the geographical margins, in much the same manner as the Irish Plantations had attempted to do with the native Irish, were just over 70 years later to send aid to Famine stricken Ireland, but not as a recognised part of the American nation in their own right.

Marx was very aware of the national revolutionary tradition in Ireland as well as Poland. In February 1848, in a speech given in Brussels to support the Polish revolution, he said:

> The Cracow revolution has given all of Europe a magnificent example by identifying the cause of nationhood with the cause of democracy and the liberation of the oppressed class ... It is finding its principles confirmed in Ireland, where the purely nationalist party has gone to the grave with O'Connell, and the new national party is above all reforming and democratic.

Just what Marx meant by "the oppressed class" in Poland at that time, where the industrial proletariat, in his terms, was only just emerging, is an interesting question, as would be what he meant by "democratic" in the case of Ireland. Marx was to arrive in London and make a closer acquaintance with the Irish revolutionary movement only after the failure of the 1848 revolutions throughout Europe. Engels had lived in Manchester from 1842-4, knew of Ireland through Irish members of the Chartist movement, and, more intimately, through a relationship with Mary Burns which began in 1843.

A kind of mythology has been built up that Marx and Engels were deeply involved with Irish revolutionary movements in England and gave them material and theoretical support. In fact there is scant evidence for this and the stubborn continuation of the tradition of a nationalist revolutionary movement among the Irish actually caused them some ideological problems. The reality over the next 20 or so years was that the natural constituency for the ideas of Marxism in Ireland was among the IRB/Fenian movement, which for Marx would undoubtedly have presented problems, both in terms of their programmes and 'terrorist' methods.

In the 1790s and early 1800s there were Corresponding Societies in England, and in Scotland the United Scotsmen, which would have regarded themselves as part of the same international current as the United Irishmen and the French revolutionaries. The London Society published an *Address to the Irish Nation* in 1798, saying:

> May Nations ... learn ... that when a people once permits Government
> to violate the genuine Principles of Liberty, Encroachment will be
> grafted upon Encroachment, ... Power will engender Power, till the
> Liberties of ALL will be held at despotic command ...

(Shades of the later Marxist idea: A nation which enslaves another cannot itself be free).

Although these Societies never rose to the height of a true revolutionary movement they did, after 1800, introduce the idea of repeal of the Act of Union to some in the British democratic movement, often literate craftsmen or tradesmen. Within a decade, into the English industrial revolution as Eric Hobsbawm said, came the Irish, with "mutual aid and kinship solidarity" - and they came in large numbers. By 1851 a quarter of the population of Liverpool had been born in Ireland.

But Hobsbawm was only partly correct in his characterisation. As well as "kinship solidarity" many immigrants brought with them their nationalist and revolutionary outlooks, not to mention membership of nationalist groupings. Many had direct family experiences of 1798 and its aftermath to draw on, some came educated and with sedition in mind.

Simultaneously, Ulster underwent its own industrialization, largely closed to Catholics, and many of the Presbyterians who left Ireland after the failure of 1798 went to the fledgling American republic. The differing religious strands of the United Irishmen never really came together again in emigration.

When in 1830s England the Chartist movement began to coalesce, among its various components was to be found this Irish current, which did not regard the Act of Union and other demands for Irish freedom as finished business. In the main these new Irish workers came from a rural Catholic background and factory life in the land of their oppressor forced many fundamental reassessments.

Among those who travelled already educated and politically aware was James Bronterre O'Brien, born in 1805 in Longford. A studious boy, he was noticed by the Edgeworth family and taken into the Edgeworth Town School, went to university in Dublin and then to London to qualify for the bar, where he met Cobbett, Hunt and other reformers. His writing skills were prodigious and he was in great demand for English radical papers. He studied the French Revolution, translating a *History of Babeuf's Conspiracy of the Equals*, which had a great influence on his thinking. He defended Robespierre against his critics, no timid thing in the England of the time, and his writings were immensely popular. Gammage (*History of the Chartist Movement*, Merlin Press, 1969) says that: "No other speaker was capable of rising to such a height, or of so impressing an audience with the strength and intensity of his feelings."

Also in England and also a barrister was Feargus O'Connor, son and nephew of United Irishmen. Margaret Cole (in *Makers of the Labour Movement*, Longmans, London, 1948) reveals how even socialists in England have succumbed to the view of Irish revolutionaries as wild and romantic, when she says:

> All his own accounts of his early life are extravagant and untrustworthy; but it is certain that he was an uncontrolled Irish lad, and instinctively agin any authority of any kind.

She points out that O'Connor's father was "a considerable landowner, a sceptic and admirer of Voltaire". Feargus experienced parliamentary politics under the Union as an MP in alliance with Daniel O'Connell. He broke with O'Connell, disagreeing with some of the deals struck with the Whigs and then became a Radical choosing, according to Gammage, "the manufacturing districts ... in which to win for himself a prominent position".

These Irishmen brought agitational, propaganda and organisational skills, learned from the national popular movements which followed 1798 in Ireland and were superior to most things around in Britain, straight to bear on the workers' movement there. They ran newspapers, organised mass meetings, put together demands and incited street warfare. In this sense they, and the many unnamed Irish immigrants who followed them, acted as revolutionary leaven in the Chartist bread. The *Northern Star*, O'Connor's paper, was the greatest mass organiser in England in the middle part of the 19th century, with a circulation of 33,000 and a readership of ten times that. O'Connor worked within Chartism from 1837 until its demise around 1852, firstly as part of its revolutionary wing and then as an electoralist. At one point he came up with a 'back to the land' scheme for the urban poor, which Cole interprets as a reversion "to the agrarianism of his

Irish youth". He was elected to Westminster, as MP for Nottingham, in 1847. His first act as an MP was to call for justice for Ireland and the repeal of the Act of Union. This had never figured strongly in his Chartist campaigns, but clearly it had never left his mind.

This role of outsider acting as the promulgator of revolutionary mass action in the metropolitan countries was to become part of the fabric of socialist political life in the decades up to the 1930s and the victory of fascism. Marx, Engels, Bakunin, Trotsky, Luxemburg, Serge, all took part in the political life of metropolitan countries other than their own. Many of these were Jewish, but the original role models were the Irish in Britain.

O'Connor and O'Brien, though, were caught in a dichotomy: able to take part in the great democratic movements in Britain, they were unable at the same time to play a real part in the struggle within Ireland against British rule. They had to choose. Their problem was similar to one described by Declan Kiberd in another context: they were "caught between a reality for which there were no obvious forms and a set of proffered forms which did not cohere with that reality". They had to convert Irishness into something which an English audience could politically understand. (Do those Protestants who want to be republicans and nationalists in the Ireland of today face the same dichotomy?).

The idea of internationalism, of being part of a greater movement than any nation within itself could provide, was certainly pregnant in the period of the late 18th century. Revolutionaries such as Paine, Jefferson and Tone travelled from country to country. But by the time of the Chartist wave this fluidity had become more difficult, as empires and colonial power had grown for the major European nations and America had settled into its own internal dynamic. Within these islands the Union seemed secure. Revolutionaries were travelling from country to country, but usually as refugees from reaction.

1848 briefly revived the old fluidity, but not in Britain where the real end of the mass Chartist movement came in the middle 1840s, just before the Irish Famine. After the collapse of the 1848 revolutions a multifaceted crisis hit all revolutionary currents in Europe, nationalist, democratic and socialist/communist alike. For a time the continuous human revolutionary thread which linked the waves of 1798 and 1848 to the latter part of the 19th century appeared to be nearly broken.

Ireland and France were among the few countries where a living revolutionary tradition could trace its continuity back over the generations. The next phase, which really began at the end of the 1860s, was part of a new rise in the European revolutionary tide, culminating in the Paris Commune. But by this time new classes: the industrial working class and certain elements of the petty bourgeoisie; new forms of organisation: trade unions, workers' parties, anarchism, the First International, were on the scene. Jacobinism had been surpassed in many countries, but in others, such as Ireland, where secret organisation was still required on a daily basis to overcome repression, the republican tradition was to provide the most fertile ground from which socialist activism could spring.

Joseph Patrick McDonnell, though, is a name that will *not* spring to the lips of many. Even James Connolly appears to have been unaware of his life and work. The son of a baker in Dublin, he went to the Catholic University but left in 1863 without a degree. About this time he began to give lectures, around the general title of 'The Past and Present of Ireland'. He found his way into the IRB and became a propagandist in its disputes with the National Brotherhood in the 1860s. In September 1865 he wrote that

> ... 'constitutional agitation' is dead, and its putrid body can never again be resuscitated ... It is a silly thing for us Irishmen to be abusing England's Government for its conduct towards us, while some of our own countrymen are our most bitter foes ... the hand of God and man may shortly be raised in defence of liberty and the old land.

McDonnell was involved in various paramilitary type activities and had links to James Stephens. He was jailed, pressured by the police, and for whatever reason, his link with the IRB was broken. He went to London in 1868 and worked, precariously, as a journalist. In 1869 he took a prominent part in the campaign for an amnesty for Fenian prisoners and helped organise the 'monster rallies' of Irish immigrants and their English sympathisers in London. Marx attended one of these, on 24th October 1869, at which McDonnell was the principal speaker. When the Paris Commune arose a committee of support was formed in London, with the Irish National Committee as a prominent part. This committee passed resolutions such as:

> ... the Irish people resident in London are duty bound ... to express their
> sympathy with their Celtic brothers of France in their heroic struggle
> against the barbarous invader, and offer them their hearty
> congratulations on the re-establishment of the republic.

The quasi-ethnic construction of this resolution appears strange, but
it acts as a cypher for views which have to be traced back to United
Irish origins. The old alliance between Irish nationalism and French
republicanism must have surged into the imaginative memories of all
those Irish emigrants in London, who would have voted *aye!*

Soon after, in Dublin and London, proposals were afoot to send an
Irish Brigade to help the Commune against its enemies and some
hundreds actually went, from both cities. McDonnell was arrested and
appeared at Bow Street Court, charged with

> unlawfully inducing persons to quit her Majesty's dominions ... in order
> that such persons might be induced to accept service in a foreign state
> at war with a friendly state.

This is not the place to relate McDonnell's subsequent work to
establish Irish sections of the First International, or his relationship
with Marx and Engels. But for the rest of his life he was an active
labour organiser, in London and then New Jersey, having very much
the same type of experiences as Connolly did some decades later.

The First International never became the directing body for workers'
movements in different countries, as Marx and Engels intended it to
be. It was mostly a corresponding and debating centre. But its
attempted introduction into Cork reveals an interesting debate between
republicans, Catholic nationalists and proto-internationalists. In early
1872 John De Morgan, a northerner with a vague biography and
probably a Fenian fellow-traveller, "... called together a few friends
and ... formed a branch of the International."

This brought the *Cork Examiner* down on their heads and created an
instant scandal. The *Constitution,* even less a friend of nationalism and
the working class, then took up the hue and cry and wrote that

> it should not be forgotten that in this country we have our illegal
> conspiracies also ... The fenians of yesterday will be the
> Internationalists of tomorrow. What matters the name. We think the

English Government might with advantage copy to some extent the vigour of the French Government in dealing with this matter.

The *Cork Examiner*, having a slightly different political complexion, ventured

that this organisation can find no foothold here. Our working classes have no sympathy with irreligion or immorality ... The leading terrorists of the French Revolution scarcely ever uttered a truculent sentiment ... And they helped to lay the seeds of that tree of brotherhood of which the International is now supposed to be the trunk ...

Soon the church joined the fray. One Canon Maguire stated that

the Internationalists had come to the wrong place in coming to Ireland, because the people of this country were too much attached to their faith to be led away by the doctrines of the International Society.

At a public meeting which ended in a riot the local Fenians made their first statement, they were expected to denounce the International, but their speaker, Daniel McCarthy, *inter alia*, said that

the men of Cork ... who in the cause of nationality were ready to make any sacrifice, would ever be found forward and foremost in maintaining their own rights ... It was a privilege which God had given man, and if the International Society enabled them to attain that object, he said to every working man "join them" ...

Then followed a further onslaught by the Catholic church, which drew one of the Fenian leaders, JFX O'Brien onto its side, declaring:

Is it not remarkable that this is the only country in which the International cannot get a footing despite all their attempts, though long since Irish nationalists were charged with being tainted with socialism and communism and everything bad? ... What can there be in common between the sacred and holy cause of Irish nationality and the hell born International? Why, even our love of country, which during so many centuries has developed a heroic patriotism unsurpassed, scarce equalled in the world's history is laughed at by the Internationals, for they recognise no distinction of country ...

This was not the view of all leading Fenians at the time. John O'Mahony wrote that:

> Thoroughly Irish though I be, I hold my allegiance to the Universal republic, founded upon the sacred principles of Fraternity, Equality, and Liberty, to be paramount to that I owe my native land ...

By the 1870s imperialist capitalism was well established on the globe. Europe had established a kind of world domination, the workers' movement, though yet to take its modern form, was growing in all the major countries and old-style Jacobinism, equated with nationalism, seemed a thing of the past, at least to Marxists. That was not the case, and is not the case. Many of the questions raised in the Enlightenment remain on the agenda.

JFX O'Brien expressed a true vein of Catholic nationalism when he denounced the International in biblical and Catholic exclusivist terms. His vision, unlike that of O'Mahony, was not a universalist one. He reflects how far some elements within Fenianism had travelled from Tone and Fitzgerald. But in this respect Ireland was both behind and in front of developments which were to occur in other countries (or sections of countries) where national oppression remained the major political problem.

Somehow, like race and gender, national oppression acts as a focus which can exert a pull on those oppressed over longer periods than class alone. The modern period has seen complex interactions between these things. The Marxist movement has attempted to give a 'universalist' answer to these problems, as the Enlightenment had before it, but in trying to subsume other forms of oppression into class struggle in a reductionist manner it has often blinded itself to the real and more complex dialectic of human history.

The First International referred to its members as Citizen: they were members of a universal workers' republic, yet to be formed. From the Second International this became Comrade: members of a movement with national mass parties which already existed. In some sense the feeling of belonging to a line which stretched back to 1789 and beyond had been symbolically broken. It was the Russians who in moments of *extremis*, would bring this submerged idea to the surface again, but the degeneration of the communist movement, centred on the Russian experience, erased it for revolutionaries of the 20th century, who were taught to trace their history back to the Commune, but no further.

Marx, certainly, wanted to create a sense of the new period in history, when the working class was to be the driving force. For much of his early life he had worked at what was really a critique of the Enlightenment and its antecedents. We can too easily forget what Marx took as positive from this tradition, only remembering what was rejected, or what might have been improperly understood. Marx was, after all, a man of his time.

The Marxist movement has never really accepted the nationalism of the oppressed as part of its own programme, even when paying it lip service or utilising it as an ally in struggle. The relationship between class, citizenship, democracy, nation and inter-nationalism has still to be re-explored theoretically by those who come from a Marxist tradition. Marx cannot be accused of not dealing with problems of democracy, state and individual freedom, the *Critique of Hegel's Philosophy of Right*, written in 1843, is precisely about these things.

But Marx, for whatever reason, did not later develop these ideas at length, except perhaps in relation to events as they occurred in 19th century politics. This work contains important statements such as

> Democracy is the solution to the riddle of all constitutions. Here the constitution is constantly ... brought back to its real basis, the real man, the real people ... The constitution appears as what it is, the free product of man ... the constitution is nothing more than one element in the being of the people ... the political constitution does not explicitly form the state ... The abstraction of the state as such belongs only to the modern time, because the abstraction of private life also belongs only to modern times.

These things are once again on the agenda globally, but at a time when the remnants of Marxism seem ill equipped to deal with them from a position of certainty. But, then again, perhaps precisely this period of uncertainty, when the dead weight of Stalinism and the dead illusion of permanent vanguardism are at their weakest, is the best time for Marxists, republicans, radical democrats and others to return to and rework the traditions of 1798 and its international and historical meanings.●

Tom Paine

The Ideas of 1798
Do They Have Any Meaning for Contemporary Unionism?

by Norman Porter

What meaning should the events of 1798 have for contemporary unionism? This may seem like a pointless question to some. Others may concede its point but decide that its only plausible answer is 'none'. And yet others may agree on its having a point but think that its best answer is 'quite a lot'. I want to argue for a version of this last response. But, first, let me say a little about the other two.

Norman Porter is an academic and author currently conducting research on Northern Ireland. He is a Senior Research Fellow at INCORE.

The question may seem pointless in the sense that it invites the wrong approach to history. If our concern is to discover the truth about the events of 1798, then to introduce concerns of contemporary unionism into the picture simply adds confusion. Or so certain historians would tell us. Here the idea is that only those whose vision is undistorted by political perceptions can deliver the authentic story of 1798.

On these terms to take my question seriously is to indulge bad history. Brian Walker says that to allow present commitments to influence our orientation to the past, is to suppose that history is appropriately "used to supply role models or simple answers" (*Dancing to History's Tune: History, myth and politics in Ireland*, p 60, Institute of Irish Studies, Belfast, 1996). Not only is this bad, he thinks, but reckless too. Or at least it is in an Irish context, where such an attitude to history frequently underpins sectarianism. Perhaps, then, the rub is this: my question should be treated as pointless, since if it isn't it becomes potentially very dangerous. Walker and those who reason like him are on to something. To reduce the complexities of the past to models and answers that simply underwrite current political prejudices produces bad history. And such bad history frequently does have dangerous implications. But that's about as much as can be conceded. What can't be admitted is the possibility of 'neutral' history, not least because the very language in which history is written or told is the language of some tradition or another. Here even professional or 'non-political' historians can't ultimately prevent prejudices acquired from their present circumstances affecting their explanations of past events.

But the real issue at stake isn't how we go about writing faithful accounts of 1798. The question I've posed has a much broader compass, one which imagines a continuing interrelation of past and present. It supposes that the meaning of 1798 is disclosed through a variety of forms, not to mention through the conflicts between them. It is revealed, for example, not just through the experiences of the United Irishmen, but also through subsequent experiences inspired by theirs; not only through their original ideas, but also through later extensions and even transformations of these ideas.

In short, the question I am focusing on only makes sense if 1798 is thought of in terms of a tradition that is ongoing and open-ended.

And it's precisely such a way of thinking that is missed by mutterings about questions of this sort being either pointless or dangerous.

This is not what is missed by those unionists and republicans who value working within a tradition. Both would see the point of the question but would typically think it allows a negative reply only. Their problem is a different one. Nonetheless it's not hard to understand the logic of their thinking. Consider for a moment a standard unionist line.

1798, far from ranking with such definitive dates in the collective unionist memory as 1690 or 1912, seems to carry negative connotations of two sorts. First, it recalls a past which almost deprived unionism of a future. Second, it anticipates a future in which unionism will be rendered redundant anyway.

On this reading, 1798 refers to a set of subversive goals that had the very real potential to destroy unionism. Had the '98 Rebellion succeeded in ending British rule in Ireland, there would not have been an Act of Union and unionism as we know it would probably never have developed. To celebrate the memory of the United Irishmen, then, seems simultaneously to lament unionism's continuing presence on Irish soil. And since such a lament can scarcely be expected of unionists neither, it appears, can such celebration.

The explicit anti-unionist overtones of 1798 are not just matters of historical curiosity, however. They appear integral to the republican tradition inspired by the United Irishmen. Many of those who trace their ideological origins to Wolfe Tone and make annual pilgrimages to Bodenstown dream, quite simply, of an Ireland united and independent. This is, of course, an Ireland in which unionism as such can have no political purchase. And it is, needless to say, just such an Ireland that unionists fear. Accordingly, 1798 can have no significance for unionists today, except as a symbol of their fears. It represents a hostile tradition. Or so it seems.

Seeming so is, however, somewhat misleading. On the foregoing reading, the significance of 1798 is reduced to the issue of British rule in Ireland, and thus to the fundamental constitutional dispute between unionism and nationalism. Sure, certain narrowly conceived unionist and republican interests may be suited by this reading, but the reductionism it entails makes for thin history and unimaginative politics. It suggests a closed tradition.

An open tradition permits a much broader interpretation of 1798's significance. And it's such an interpretation I now wish to press for. I want to suggest that 1798 contains considerable meaning for contemporary unionism. This meaning is communicated through three specific challenges, which don't so much threaten unionism's existence, as ask searching questions of what it stands for.

One challenge is that of recapturing the progressive, anti-sectarian ideals of 1798. No doubt this is a challenge for all political persuasions in Ireland today, but it is a particularly poignant one for unionism. To see why requires posing stark questions about the dissenting tradition which championed the ideals of 1798 and which subsequently became unionism's main constituency.

Why was it that ideas central to the American and French revolutions, and, more generally, to the Enlightenment - ideas which clearly inspired a generation of dissenters - especially in Belfast - proved to have such a short tenure? Why, in particular, did they become marginalised so effortlessly within dissenting circles?

All sorts of answers are possible here. Perhaps commitment to these ideas weakened as dissenters' material interests were increasingly satisfied. Perhaps the ideas were too tamely held to withstand the sectarian divisions that started to appear among the United Irishmen and escalated following the Act of Union. Or perhaps the ideas only ever had a slender chance of surviving, since they took little root beyond the educated circles of the United Irishmen's leadership.

Answers like these all have a point. But, despite them, this unsettling thought remains: the ideas that turned much of Europe upside down and drove a generation of Irish dissenters to take enormous risks seem subsequently to have been cast aside too cheaply for comfort. Worse still, there is the shocking truth that ideas that were (at the very least) anti-sectarian in nature were generally swapped within dissenting circles for ideas that fitted within a sectarian mould. This seems to me the crucial and truly disturbing point.

Even if we can find reasons why, by the time of Gladstone's First Home Rule Bill, most dissenters identified with the cause of unionism, these reasons don't tell us all we need to know. They don't tell us why so many dissenters complied, either meekly or enthusiastically, with the Orange and Tory prescriptions with which the unionist cause (to its great discredit) has for so long been saddled. It's not enough here to blame Catholicism's attempted hijacking of all things Irish, for this implies that one kind of sectarianism can only be met by another. We are confronted, rather, with a very discomfiting loss of political and moral orientation within the dissenting tradition.

For the sake of the Union, dissenters were for the most part willing to forfeit their radical, anti-sectarian ideals: ideals that had fired the imaginations of their forebears and had given brief promise of a better future for all of us on this island. The challenge now is for unionism to rediscover what it lost, as memory of 1798 receded in the dissenter consciousness and was replaced by memories of a different kind.

This is to appropriate 1798 for unionism. It is to prioritise anti-sectarianism in a way that effectively dislodges the privileged place Orangeism continues to enjoy within unionist ranks. Facing up to the challenge of 1798 demands nothing less.

In truth it demands a good deal more. To capture and sustain the anti-sectarian legacy of 1798 involves taking up another challenge, namely that of re-articulating a citizen-centred politics. For the United Irishmen such a politics was entailed in the cardinal ideas of the French Revolution - liberty, equality and fraternity. These ideas were central to the vindication of citizen dignity against hierarchical systems of privilege and domination. And they were crucial to the moves of treating the 'people' as the source of political power, and of defining the people as 'citizens' rather than as subjects.

Now, it is true to say that notions of citizen dignity and self-rule as well as ideas of liberty, equality and fraternity seem less radical to us than they did to the United Irishmen. In a sense they comprise part of the taken-for-granted background against which much of our politics is conducted. But to suppose that is all they do is short-sighted. A serious, citizen-centred mode of politics continues to need fresh translations. And it continues to challenge many of our priorities and practices, not least those familiar to unionism. There is, for example, considerably more to developing a common sense of citizenship than unionism typically acknowledges. For unionists it is enough that all citizens in the North are in principle granted the same procedural entitlements. But this isn't enough at all. What is required in addition is the creation of social and cultural conditions conducive to the cultivation of a shared civic identity among citizens.

In the divided society that is Northern Ireland, this is only possible through a concerted standing against religiously-based segregation in areas of housing, education and the like. Also required is the creation of public institutions capable of commanding the allegiance of all citizens, and not just members of one tradition. To pay more than lip-service to these requirements would transform the priorities and practices of unionists (and others). It would breathe radical life back into the citizen-centred emphases of 1798. And a unionism that accepted the challenge here would give unprecedented promise of a new political future for us all.

It is of course naive to suppose that such a future is possible without unionism facing a third challenge from 1798, that of affirming Irishness. Part of the difficulty here, however, is knowing what this should involve.

For some it involves nothing less than strict adherence to the United Irishmen's convictions that British rule in Ireland must be ended, and that religious divisions can be transcended through an affirmation of our common nationality. The trouble with this rendering is that it fails to account for three things: (1) that there is a difference in kind between a British government (now) that declares it has no selfish strategic or economic interest in Ireland and one (then) that imposed its rule in arbitrary, corrupt and despotic ways; (2) that, unfortunately, Irishness stopped being a cure for sectarianism the moment it was colonised by Catholicism; and (3) that it is far-fetched to expect unionists to consent to their own extinction.

A more realistic rendering of the challenge might go something like this: It is implausible to regard the North simply as a site of the Union. It should be regarded, rather, as a site where British and Irish factors intermingle and clash and demand mutual recognition. Accordingly, unionism should stop defining Britishness and Irishness in oppositional terms. Irishness (like Britishness) should be accommodated within Northern Ireland and within North-South bodies.

Although more modest, this rendering still challenges two dominant tendencies within unionism: the Ulster Protestant particularism exemplified by Ian Paisley and various loyalist paramilitaries, and mainstream unionism's demeaning craving for recognition by the British establishment. A re-appropriation of the Irishness of all of us on this island and a determination to give it its due would help ease unionism out of the defensive mindset in which it has been stuck for too long.

To conclude, a unionism that responded positively to the challenges of the United Irishmen by moving beyond sectarianism, prioritising citizenship and accommodating Irishness would offer rare hope to us all, North and South. That it's even possible to speculate on its doing so attests to the lasting power of the legacy of 1798.●

Samuel Neilson from County Down
A founder of the United Irishmen

111

Bartholomew Teeling, aide-de-camp to General Humbert

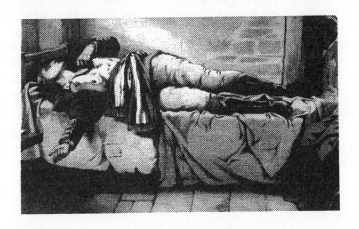

Dissenting From 'Catholic-Nationalism'
Wolfe Tone As a Role Model

By Carol Coulter

One of my earliest memories which began a realisation of Ireland's political and religious differences is of an incident which occurred when I was a child attending national school in the West of Ireland in the 1950s. It was a beautiful sunny day and my mother, the teacher in the one-teacher local Church of Ireland school, who also acted as the school transport scheme, had left me to walk the mile or so home while she detoured to take a group of children to their home some three miles away.

Carol Coulter is a journalist with *The Irish Times* and the author of a number of books and essays on nationalism, feminism and social questions.

The walk took me past a small roadside Marian shrine, erected a few years earlier in the Marian Year. As I passed it a group of boys, much bigger than I was, were going home in the opposite direction from the Catholic school. "Why didn't you bless yourself?" one demanded. I didn't answer. I knew that one of the differences between my family and our Catholic neighbours was that we did not worship the Virgin Mary as they did, and we thought it wrong, but I also knew that we avoided confrontation on this and other religious issues.

"Are you not a Catholic?" They persisted. "What are you? Are you a Protestant? Who are you?" The last question seemed particularly menacing, as if they wanted to pursue the question of my deviance further. After about five minutes they tired of their fruitless interrogation and walked on, and I continued my walk home with a thumping heart.

It must be said that such incidents were very rare. I did not know these boys, and among our neighbours my family's religious affiliation never stood in the way of a close intimacy forged from generations of mutual dependence and support in an area ravaged by the privations of landlordism and the difficulties of survival on poor land. Many families, including mine, had experienced eviction and involvement in the Land League, and an awareness of this shared history underlay the strong bonds of social solidarity which were a mark of that community.

But that history was not unproblematic in Protestant national schools. We followed a history course, and history textbooks, identical to those in Catholic national schools. These represented Irish history as a prolonged struggle to remove a British and Protestant yoke in order to create an Irish Catholic state. The Republic of Ireland of the 1950s was, we were taught, the realisation of that struggle.

In the periods time-tabled for religious instruction, however, we learned of the errors of the Church of Rome. While it was wrong that Catholics had not been allowed practice their religion - or own a horse, or inherit land, or suffer any of the other discriminations of the Penal Laws - this did not mean their religion was right. We Protestants magnanimously believed they had the right to worship as they chose, even if they were wrong. This slightly condescending attitude sustained us when we were corralled behind the gates of the school on Corpus Christi. Apart from the monthly livestock fair in the town, when they were closed against marauding animals, this was the only day of the year that the gates of the school were closed, a day when we sharply felt our difference, that some sort of question mark lay over our membership of the community, over our entitlement to co-own our shared history.

But I knew that they were wrong. Almost as soon as I started to learn Irish history I realised that the interpretation just did not match the facts. No individual brought that home more than Wolfe Tone.

Tone was, we were taught, a young Protestant who attended Trinity College ('our' university). Inspired by indignation at the iniquities of English rule, and generously outraged by discrimination against his Catholic fellow-countrymen, he turned his back on the privileges his religious background could have brought him and sought to unite "Catholic, Protestant and Dissenter in the common name of Irishman" in opposition to English rule. In so doing he had the support of other Protestants, many from the north, like Henry Joy McCracken, whose name rolled so musically off the tongue. They, too, were Protestants like us. So this was very much a Protestant enterprise.

We learned of Tone's work to organise the United Irishmen, his hopes for French help, the doomed expeditions sent from France, including that to nearby Killala, and imagined the French marching along the familiar roads on their way to Castlebar and thence to Longford. The surrounding area was suffused with memories of the '98 Rebellion - the main street in Tubbercurry, where I went to school, is Teeling Street, and outside my mother's home town of Colloooney there is a statue of Bart Teeling. As we passed it she would describe how an English gunner was placed on the hill behind where the statue now stood, and he was shooting at the insurgents as they marched along the road. Bart Teeling broke from the body of the rebel troop and galloped up the hill in the teeth of the gunfire to shoot the English gunner dead. The image of the young rider, the sound of his horse's hooves, the cheer when the gun fell silent, were all vivid as she recounted the story.

The came the tragic *dénouement* - Tone captured in a French ship and sentenced to death, the small-minded English refusal to recognise his rank as a French officer, his death on board ship in tragic circumstances. We knew the rebellion continued in far-off Wexford, where a priest led the insurgents before it petered out, but with the death of Tone the romance had gone out of it, to revive, briefly, in the Emmet rebellion of 1803.

Was it a subversive nuance in Protestant schools which gave those Protestant rebels an aura of glamour, with their stirring declarations, their foreign allies, and the tragic wives and lovers they left behind, compared with the undoubtedly brave but, to us, essentially distant figure of Father Murphy? Or was it the physical proximity of Killala, and the familiarity of the route the French took, which made their involvement in '98, at the behest of Wolfe Tone, somehow more real than that of 'the boys of Wexford'?

Whatever it was, the place occupied by Wolfe Tone and the other leaders of 1798 allowed Protestants in the independent Irish state - or at least the part of it I grew up in - to co-own the heritage of republicanism. The children from the Catholic schools in the town could parade all they liked on Corpus Christi, Wolfe Tone was mine in a way he would never be theirs. Their heroes really belonged to me, they could only be borrowed by those Catholic children who thought they were more Irish than I was. I could identify with them in a way they could not, I could take pride in their freely entered into alliance with the downtrodden Catholics of Irish history, who rightly deserved an end to discrimination, but whose struggle was consummated and whose leadership was enriched by the heroes my people had provided. Catholic emancipation was only a part of this struggle for Irish independence which had drawn everyone in Ireland into its broad sweep.

Growing up on a farm with no neighbouring children of my own age meant I had to live in my imagination to a greater extent than children in an urban environment. Such a rural upbringing also undoubtedly gave me an identification with the land that, again, seems absent from the experience of children in cities and towns. Both combined to give a resonance to the appeal of the version of Irish nationalism promulgated, with all the contradictions I have described, in the national school system of the 1950s. Added to this was the existence of nationalist role models from my own community (including Constance Markiewicz from the north of my county, who came from an Ascendancy background but who rejected it) which allowed me to gain a sense of that nationalism as a broad and inclusive movement, while realising that many did not see it this way.

I later learned of the intensive 'Catholic-nationalist' indoctrination my contemporaries were receiving in their national and later secondary schools. So pervasive was it, apparently, that beatings by the Christian Brothers, or more subtle tortures by the nuns; intimidating, if not outright abusive, subordination to an all-powerful priesthood; and an atavistic, quasi-racist nationalism combined seamlessly to oppress a whole generation and provoke in many of its members a hatred for the whole package. I do not doubt that for many people this was indeed their experience. But I have often wondered how on earth they were taught any Irish history at all, and certainly the history of 1798 and its leaders, without some acknowledgement of the generous, liberal, freethinking spirit which inspired it.

The 'Catholic-nationalist' label, so often used as an epithet by Eoghan Harris and those influenced by him, to me was always so patently an oxymoron, it seemed difficult to reconcile it with even a cursory acquaintance with historical fact.

The year 1968 probably acted as a beacon for young revolutionaries and radicals in Europe in much the same way as the French Revolution did in its day. Certainly, in the years that followed 1968 students were fired with hopes for the transformation of the world as we knew it, inspired with the ideals of international solidarity, and confident our generation would change the world. When I read the *Autobiography* of Wolfe Tone in the immediate aftermath of 1968 it was like reading the words of a contemporary. His irreverence, his contempt for the dogma of religion and indifference to distinctions of race or religious denomination, his burning enthusiasm for revolutionary change, his passionate affection for his friends and love for his wife, his fondness for good food, wine and the opera all seemed powerfully subversive of the values which had dominated us and which we were now trying to overthrow.

In all the commemorative material on Wolfe Tone so far produced, his great humour and humanity seem to be losing out. Yet these are things which make him so attractive a figure, and make his life and work so real.

His *Autobiography* has not, to my knowledge, been republished since 1937, when an abridged edition was edited by Seán Ó Faoláin. It would do more to dispel any idea that 1798 was a sectarian affair, or that Catholicism owned Irish republicanism, than any amount of historical debate. I cannot end without a few quotes from it to demonstrate just how appropriate a hero Wolfe Tone is for anyone who adheres to the values of tolerance and humanity, and seeks a world of true liberty, equality and fraternity.

In his second visit to Belfast, in July 1792, he describes his worries that his demand for Catholic emancipation will not be included in the declaration to be drawn up. The entry for July 13th reads:

> The Harpers again. Strum, Strum and be hanged. Hear that several Catholics have been seen; run to try; find Magog, Weldon and others to a large amount. The hair of Dr Halliday's wig miraculously grows grey with fear of the Catholics. Several comets appear in the marketplace. Walk the Catholics about to show them the lions. See the figure of Commerce at the insurance office; the Catholics mistake it for an image, and kneel down, take out their beads and say their prayers before it; leave them at the Exchange and go to dinner with Simms ...
>
> July 19th. Sunday. Go to Mass; foolish enough; too much trumpery. The King of France dethroned!! Very glad of it, for now the people will have fair play.

Much of the *Autobiography* deals with his visit to France and his attempts to persuade the French government to send an expedition to Ireland, punctuated by his descriptions of food, wine, women and the opera. But he is homesick for Ireland, his friends and especially his wife and family. "March17th. St Patrick's Day. Dined *alone* in the Champs Elysées. Sad! Sad!"

He finds "the French women before the English, far and wide", and either London or Paris the places to go for "casual fruition", but urges readers "if you wish to be happy, choose a companion from home," and his devotion to his wife is never in doubt. In his writing about sex it is as if the years of Victorian prudery and the repression in Ireland during the first half of this century never came into being:

> July 4th. I want to change my domicile. I am lodged in the house of a little 'bossue' (Anglicé, a hunchback) and she wants me to go to bed to her, and I won't, for my virtue forbids it, and so she is out of humour and very troublesome sometimes. To tell the God's truth, I have no great merit in my resistance, for she is as crooked as a ram's horn (which is a famous illustration) and as ugly as sin besides. Rot her, the dirty little faggot, she torments me. ●

Alternative Enlightenments
The United Irishmen, Cultural Diversity and the Republic of Letters

by Luke Gibbons

> We will not buy or borrow liberty from America or France,
> but manufacture it ourselves, and work it up with those materials
> which the hearts of Irishmen furnish them with at home ...
> *Address of the United Irishmen to the Scottish Convention, 1793*

1998 is an appropriate year not only to commemorate the ideals of the United Irishmen, but also the coming of age of the Enlightenment, as represented by figures such as Thomas Jefferson (1743-1825) in America, Immanuel Kant (1724-1804) in Germany and Voltaire (1694-17780 in France. If the legacy of the Enlightenment retains any validity at the end of the 20th century, it may help to remind us that a culture has not found its own voice until it has expressed itself in a body of critical as well as creative work. "It is one thing for a race to produce artistic material", the great African-American thinker WEB du Bois wrote, "it is quite another thing for it to produce the ability to interpret and criticize this material".

Luke Gibbons lectures in the School of Communications at Dublin City University. Among his published work is *Transformations in Irish Culture* (CUP 1996).

This is a lesson that countries with strong traditions of anti-intellectualism, such as Ireland, can ill afford to ignore. So far from being secondary to the work of art, the centrality of criticism is such that while a creative voice may readily be granted, as a kind of poetic licence, to dispossessed or marginal cultures, the critical mediation of the resultant artworks is less easily devolved onto the cultures that produce them.

Art can assume vernacular forms, or speak in a regional accent, but criticism, and intellectual enquiry in general, remain firmly located in the metropolitan centre. Ireland has produced leading literary figures such as James Joyce, WB Yeats and Sam Beckett, but where are the equivalents of Adorno, Barthes or de Beauvoir, or, for that matter, Marx, Wollstonecraft or Weber? The reason for this, according to the German philosopher Edmund Husserl (1859-1938) in his famous Vienna lecture of 1935, is that while all cultures were free to express themselves mythically, religiously or creatively, only the advanced metropolitan countries of Europe had the capacity to produce theory, or modes of thought consistent with the ordinances of universal reason.

Much of what passes for contemporary critiques of the Enlightenment in recent postmodern theory and criticism is levelled at such universal pretensions on the part of western thought, but it may well be that by construing the Enlightenment almost exclusively in European terms, postmodern critics such as Michel Foucault (1926-84) and Jean-Francois Lyotard may themselves be guilty of the very Eurocentrism they deplore in others. Many reasons have been adduced for the discrediting of key Enlightenment concepts, such as a belief in historical progress and in universal schemes for human emancipation, but pre-eminent among them is their association with westernization and cosmopolitanism. Hence their lack of relevance for one of the most significant shifts in international politics, the process of decolonization, which has given rise to an upsurge in nationalism, and the growth of over 100 new nation states in the post World War Two era. It is precisely because of the West's conviction that it has a monopoly on human progress that so many anti-colonial struggles feel impelled to renounce Enlightenment ideals, thereby retreating into the cul-de-sacs of romanticism and nostalgia at the best or, at the worst, fundamentalism, sectarianism and ethnic cleansing.

Decentering the Enlightenment

In his book, *The Black Atlantic*, Paul Gilroy has remarked that for some black cultures "the enthusiasm of 1789" may relate more to the slave rebellion in Port Au Prince in Haiti than it does to revolutionary Paris. It is this possibility of alternative Enlightenments, in the periphery rather than in the imperial heartlands or the metropolitan centre, which is of interest in relation to Irish culture.

One powerful intellectual tradition which lends itself to this project, and which influenced the United Irishmen in ways yet to be fully explored, is the 18th century Scottish Enlightenment, with its overt attacks on the sovereignty of reason and its replacement by the 'man of feeling'. The cult of sensibility and its attendant ethics of sympathy and 'fellow-feeling' advocated by David Hume (1711-76) and Adam Smith (1723-90) may have contributed as much to the abolition of slavery, for instance, as the more abstract 'rights of man' espoused by American and French republicanism - though, in the last instance, Smith's and John Millar's (1725-1801) arguments about the economic inefficiency of slavery may have carried more weight.

However, whilst it was helping to abolish slavery, the Scottish Enlightenment did not hold out much hope for African, or any other oppressed cultures, wishing to throw off the shackles of colonialism. Instead, by espousing a philosophy of progress which established a clear hierarchy among cultures, and identifying that progress in turn with the advancement of political economy and British civilization, Scottish versions of liberty offered as little to the people of Port au Prince as the erstwhile French revolutionaries who suppressed the slave's rebellion in Haiti. It is this process, whereby progress acts as pretext for colonization, which the United Irishmen called into question, and which remains one of their lasting contributions to republican political thought.

One of the reasons that the Enlightenment - whether in its liberal democratic or in its more radical Marxist versions - has come to be identified with westernization, and political aggrandisement, is precisely the weakness of its critique of colonialism. Thus the abolition of colonial slavery was motivated more by Christian benevolence and philanthropy (however high-minded) than by a determination to abolish to abolish the evils of colonialism itself.

Under this dispensation, universal ideals of human rights extended to individuals but not to cultures: while all human beings were equal, some cultures were less equal than others, and their destruction was justified in the name of social improvement and development. For this reason, the remit of the American *Declaration of Independence* in 1776 did not include Indians, and when, under assimilationist policies, the native American was belatedly allowed to enter civil society, it was not as a native but as everyman, an abstract individual stripped of his or her distinctive cultural heritage.

Even Marx was not immune to this Western prejudice, arguing that in many respects, British colonialism was a progressive force in Asia, helping to break down "Chinese walls of obscurantism". This revealed a dark side of the Enlightenment, in which that blueprint for human emancipation ran perilously close to prescriptions for ethnocide - the belief that some cultures were doomed to disappear from history.

The Culture of Obsolescence

The criteria of this 'obsolescence' were varied, but from an Irish point of view at the end of the 18th century, two loomed ominously over the political landscape. This had the effect of forcing the United Irishmen, to redefine the Enlightenment in a way that pre-empts many of the strictures directed at dominant, western models of progress by contemporary postmodern or postcolonial theorists The first criterion of obsolescence in Enlightenment thought had to do with a belief that the principal obstruction to the march of progress and universal reason was a reliance on tradition, and an adherence to local or vernacular culture. It is true that the United Irishmen, in a number of declarations, set their faces firmly against the past, but Roy Foster and other historians have erroneously taken this to mean the old Irish or Gaelic order.

In fact, as Nancy Curtin and Kevin Whelan have shown, it was the British past which was the target of their invective, particularly the slavish belief in the accumulated wisdom of the British constitution over the centuries. This radical break with British common law and the heritage of the 'free-born Englishman' marked the point of no return, transforming the United Irishman from being a reformist, Whig inspired movement, akin to the Volunteers, into a fully-fledged revolutionary organization. It was figures such as Arthur O'Connor (1763-1852), Thomas Russell (1767-1803), and particularly the emigres of the New York United Irishmen as represented by William Sampson (1764-1836), Samuel Neilson(1761-1803) and William James MacNeven (1763-1841), who did most to expose the delusions of grandeur entertained by worshippers of the venerable British constitution. Sampson ridiculed English imputations of barbarism to the Irish language and Gaelic culture, stating that the clotted language of the British legal system, as eulogized by Sir William Blackstone (1723-80) and Sir Edward Coke (1552-1634), puts the Irish language to shame:

> Indeed, (he wrote) some of the very acts of parliament, enacting penalties against those that spake Irish, or dwelt among the Irishry, are such a queer compound of Danish, Norman, hog-latin and I know not what, as to be the most biting satires upon the Englishry, and those that spake English.

As for the much lauded longevity of the divinely-inspired ancient constitution, "all I will say of it", wrote Sampson, "is that the same panegyric will apply *totidem verbis* to the institutions of our red brethren, the Iroquois".

It is important to realize that Sampson's mockery of British claims to superiority over alleged primitive cultures is not inspired by the kind of backward-looking romanticism which denies progress and universality. This was the form of cultural relativism, influenced by primitivism and localism, which led German social philosophers such as Herder (1744-1803) to opt out of the Enlightenment altogether, but Sampson's defence of cultural rights is republican through and through. Like individuals, cultures are not a law unto themselves, but are also to be judged by their respect for human rights. Nonetheless, cultures are endowed with rights, and by thus associating cultural diversity with justice, the United Irishmen helped to lay the basis for a formidable anti-colonial critique within Enlightenment thought.

The second aspect of allegedly inferior cultures which justified their subjugation to, if not destruction by, advanced western powers was the persistence of superstition, which in an Irish context, of course, was shorthand for priestcraft and popery. Central to this was a belief

123

that Catholics, as Catholics, were unfit to for citizenship and for membership of the public sphere. While this interdiction against superstition was issued in the name of universal or scientific reason, its secularism was somewhat compromised by the fact that the critique of superstition did not extend to other equally irrational doctrines, such as belief in the spiritual or the supernatural. What was at stake here was not irrationality as such but a prejudice against popular or communal practices, in favour of the interiorization of 'inner faith' and private belief on the part of the individual.

Lifting the Spectre of Sectarianism

This hostility to custom and tradition in the 18th century found its expression in Protestantism, or rather in a supremacist British variant, which, as Linda Colley has argued in her book *Britons: Forging the Nation 1707-1837*, deemed Catholicism to be incompatible with Britishness itself. For Wolfe Tone, the fact that the French Revolution emanated from a Catholic culture such as France was sufficient to take the political anathema off Catholic participation in public life. His landmark publication of 1791, *An Argument on Behalf of the Catholics of Ireland*, thereby placed him outside the pale of Britishness, and on a separatist path which led irrevocably to one of the first systematic critiques of colonial rule in Enlightenment thought.

Nor were the benefits of this critique confined to Ireland in a narrow nationalist sense, as can be seen if we revert once more to the example set by the New York United Irishmen. In 1812, in a landmark case in American legal history centering on the secrecy of the Catholic confessional, William Sampson, in his professional capacity as a lawyer, made a crucial contribution towards establishing the constitutional basis for the free exercise of religious worship in the United States. As the legal historian Walter J Walsh describes it:

> (This) event ranks as perhaps the earliest recorded instance of impact litigation in American constitutional history - a test case in which an insular minority deliberately sought to appropriate the courts to transform the political structure of American society.

Sampson's argument was that the discrimination against Catholicism in American law was a residue of its Anglo-Saxon heritage, a kind of of colonial repression permitted in Ireland under the British constitution in Ireland but which had no place in a constitution truly devoted to liberty.

The Twilight of the Northern Star

It would be reassuring to think that there was no longer a need to draw attention to these innovations in political culture, but if a recent publication presenting the intellectual case for Unionism in Northern Ireland is anything to go by, it would seem that the rays of the 18th century Enlightenment have now dimmed considerably. Throughout the book, *The Idea of the Union: Statements and Critiques in Support of the Union of Great Britain and Northern Ireland*, (ed. John Wilson Foster, Belcouver Press, 1995), defenders of the British way of life make it clear that in any ethnic equation, Britishness must always be in a superior position. Irishness is essentially an inferior, if not a foreign culture, despite the fact that over 40 per cent of the population in Northern Ireland claim to be Irish.

Much is made of the multi-cultural nature of the United Kingdom, with minority cultures enjoying a whole range of freedoms, but the possibility of Britishness itself being accommodated as one identity among others within another multi-cultural formation, is simply ruled out as unthinkable. The critic John Wilson Foster writes that:

> Unionism is not just a tradition to be accommodated in a united separate Ireland like some quaint folk custom: it is a cultural reality which cannot breathe the air of Irish republican separatism from which it is bigger.

Indeed, it was bigger, having a whole empire at its disposal at the turn of the century, and it is perhaps these ingrained habits of authority which ultimately inform his belief in "the superiority of Unionism over republicanism".

Denials of elementary cultural parity are even more apparent in the pronouncements of the political scientist Richard English in the same publication: "the notion that pluralism on the British model can work in Northern Ireland seems to me to be extremely naive", he writes, for "to afford equal respect, legitimacy, and validity to the dominant cultures in the region: Protestant/unionist on the one hand, Catholic/ nationalist on the other" is "fundamentally incoherent". To see these ideas in practice, we have only to witness the triumphalism of the Orange Order at Drumcree in recent years, a fitting location for the burial of the advanced Protestant conceptions of liberty and equality bequeathed by the United Irishmen.

If the universality of reason and human rights are to retain their relevance at the end of the 20th century, then a good start could be made by renouncing such forms of ethnic absolutism, and according different cultures the same rights as individuals. Writing in support of his view that the United Irishmen "were little concerned with what we would regard as the Catholic perception of Irish nationality", the historian ATQ Stewart observes:

> The United Irishmen were patriots in the Jeffersonian sense, which is almost the opposite of ours. Men of this stamp actually regarded nationalism as uncivilized. To be a patriot was to adopt a wider, more cosmopolitan outlook, supporting the Rights of Man in opposition to the narrow self -interest of national governments.

Not least of the remarkable aspects of this statement is that it is not even true of Thomas Jefferson, let alone the United Irishmen. In common with many Enlightenment intellectuals, Jefferson was captivated by the cult of the Ossianic poems which inspired the first 'Celtic' revival in the 18th century, and went so far as to propose learning Gaelic, requesting "a grammar and a dictionary" to read Ossian in the original (a more difficult task than Jefferson imagined, given that James Macpherson, the Scottish writer who launched Ossian onto an unsuspecting public in the 1760s, never produced the originals of his so-called translations).

This invocation of a Celtic past, however imaginary, is an important corrective to the view that the 'universalism' of the Enlightenment was incompatible with the more local attachments of nationalism and native culture. In its contemporary form, this erasure of cultural difference is akin to the argument that to be liberal and progressive, not to mention being socialist or revolutionary, is to reject one's national language, music, games, or indeed any kind of distinctive cultural identity.

On this reckoning the Enlightenment is the sole preserve of citizens of the world, whereas the backward look is the fate of the benighted native, unable to let go of time and place.

The most enduring legacy of the United Irishmen is to question these redundant oppositions, refracting the Enlightenment itself through the prism of cultural diversity, and bringing a much needed colloquy of voices to the republic of letters. ●

Counsel to the Worldly-Wise

Go A-Foot and go A-head!
    That's the way to prosper;
Whoso must be carriage-led
    Suffereth serious loss per
Day in health as well as wealth,
    By that laziness with which
        Walkers have from birth warred;
And ere long grim Death by stealth
    Mounts the tilbury, and the rich
        Loller tumbleth earthward!

Also keep your conscience pure -
    Neither lie nor borrow;
He who starves to-day, be sure
    Always carves to-morrow.
March in front; don't sulk behind;
    Dare to live, though sneering groups
        Dub you *rara avis* -
"Serve your country - love your kind,"
    And whene're your spirit droops,
        Think of Thomas Davis!

James Clarence Mangan

Plaque showing the death of Father Michael Murphy at Arklow

The Significance of the 1798 Commemoration

The Lessons History Can Teach

by Martin Mansergh

In his memoirs Miles Byme wrote :

> I trust that one day, when poor Ireland will be free, that there will be a monument raised to the memory of those brave men who so heroically contributed to gain the battle of Enniscorthy.

It is very appropriate that Enniscorthy, which was the epicentre of the 1798 Rebellion in Wexford, should be the town that will be home to the National 1798 Centre.

Martin Mansergh is a special advisor to the Taoiseach, Bertie Ahern.
This essay is derived from talks given at Enniscorthy and the Slieve Gullion Winter School.

I would like to praise all those local and national historians who have helped to pin down what happened, why, when, where, and who was involved. There are local people who know what happened over every inch of the ground in 1798, almost as if it were yesterday.

To certain places a strong aura of history is attached, irrespective of how later generations or historians perceive the events that took place there. Let me draw a very imperfect analogy. In certain parts of the Western Highlands of Scotland and in the Isle of Skye, memories of Bonnie Prince Charlie, the clans who fought and died with him, and the brutality of 'Butcher' Cumberland, linger over the heather. But what is less well known is that four out of the seven companions who landed with him were Irish.

The modern historian may come along, and tell you what a total disaster the prince was, with chapter and verse. But it makes not a blind bit of difference. The legend lives on.

In Wexford in 1798 the people rose only after great provocation. They were the first to bear the full brunt in modern times of the fight for Irish freedom and independence. As in most wars and revolutions, there was a good deal of confusion along with the intensity. There was heroism, there was bloodshed, there was tragedy, and some terrible things were done on different sides, often despite the best intentions of responsible leaders. In commemorating those who fought, those who died, and those who innocently and unjustly suffered on all sides, we are not called upon to approve everything that was done in the name of freedom, order or religion, or to justify all the horrors of war and atrocities, which were repudiated by humane leaders on either side at the time. But we can and should feel a sympathy, informed by the best historical knowledge, for the fellow human-beings caught up in these events, often almost entirely involuntarily, a sympathy for the hopes and fears of those who lived through times that have left their mark on our country and our history to this day.

1798 will be commemorated at national level with the support of the Government. Many parts of the country played a prominent role in the events of the 1790s or in 1798. There was a Republic proclaimed in Connacht as well as Wexford. A Committee of Public Safety was established in Ballymena, which has been described by ATQ Stewart as "a crude form of Republican Government". In the 1790s the political and intellectual corridor between Dublin and Belfast was alive as never before or since. The United Irishmen were founded in Belfast in 1791. If one were to put a date on when it all began, I would choose the two days in May 1795, on the Cave Hill overlooking Belfast, where Wolfe Tone and his Belfast companions took a solemn obligation not to rest till they had broken the connection with Britain and asserted our country's independence. Looked at from the perspective of today, it is a real paradox that the birthplace of Irish separatism took place in Belfast, amongst ancestors of those who would nowadays mostly be counted as belonging to a different political and cultural tradition.

There is an interest in the commemoration in many different parts of the country. The Linenhall Library, whose first librarian was Thomas Russell, one of the closest friends of Wolfe Tone, is mounting a travelling exhibition. The Ulster Museum will also stage an exhibition. At the inauguration of President Mary McAleese, I met the Unionist Councillor, Harvey Bicker of Ballinahinch (where one of the main northern battles took place), who is the chairperson of the County Down 1798 Commemoration Committee. The history that we are commemorating is woven into the landscape and into the people, whose descendants live not only throughout Ireland but in America, Britain and Australia. I remember in 1988 visiting with the then Taoiseach, Charles Haughey, the Waverley Memorial near Sydney, which commemorates Michael Dwyer and the other men of 1798. Much of the early history and ballads of Australia record the experience of those transported mainly for political reasons. In the United States, Thomas Addis Emmet, brother of Robert, played a leading part in creating real civil and religious liberty in New York State, from which later Irish immigrants at the time of the Famine and afterwards would benefit. He remained inspired by the ideals of the United Irishmen, which he regarded as related to the ideals of Tom Paine and Thomas Jefferson.

The 1798 Rebellion made a permanent and indelible contribution to the evolution of the Irish diaspora. 1798 is part of the local and national heritage. We can learn much of use and relevance to our day, whatever view we take of those events. Our task today, like that which the United Irishmen set themselves, is to transcend the conflicts of the past, as we try to construct a future hoped for by many of our ancestors, but which was denied them.

131

Miles Byrne of Wexford also wrote in his memoirs:

> The United Irish laboured for nothing but civil and religious liberty for Irishmen of all persuasions, and for the independence of their country.

While the Nationalist and Republican traditions have tended to claim 1798 for their own, the fact is that 1798 is also part of the mainstream Presbyterian tradition, most of whose members would now see themselves as Unionist. Many of their ancestors had their reforming democratic ideals fulfilled. This relates perhaps to the very different experience of the two communities in the intervening years.

Padraig Pearse wrote, in *The Spiritual Nation*:

> If we accept the definition of Irish freedom as 'the Rights of Man   in Ireland', we shall find it difficult to imagine an apostle of Irish freedom who is not a democrat.

Today, like Mary Wollstonecraft and Mary Anne McCracken in the 1790s, we would speak of 'the rights of woman' as well as 'the rights of man', and Pearse himself fully endorsed the full political equality of men and women. But what his comment underlines is that the Republican tradition, inherited from 1798, 1848 or 1916, saw itself fundamentally as a democratic one. Historically, those revolts were the result of repression and exasperation with the denial or delay of democratic rights by a more powerful Government. It was not a rejection of democracy, but a case of people who believed they were being denied their democratic rights.

In our own day, conflict has arisen from a failure over three quarters of a century to reconcile the valid and conflicting rights of two main communities within the narrow internal political framework of Northern Ireland. Conflict itself has not resolved the problem, nor will any reversion to 'what we know best'. The peace process and the negotiations now underway are perhaps the first serious political effort ever to provide an accommodation between two main communities and traditions, to resolve as far as is possible at this time conflicting claims of allegiance between Ireland and Britain, and to establish at the least what the SDLP has called 'equality of allegiance'.

132

The bicentenary of 1798 is a very important one, particularly coming as it does in a year when important peace negotiations could reach a decisive phase. It is an opportunity, in effect, to go back to the beginnings of modern democratic politics in Ireland, to look at the greater fluidity of positions in the 1790s, side by side with deep-seated inter-communal tensions, which continue to this day. We should look at the 1790s as a whole, at the political movements that were born then, and especially the United Irishmen, rather than just the military climax of rebellion. *What* people wanted to achieve *politically* as well as the different *ways* they set about achieving it are equally important.

The Irish Government is supporting the Commemoration of 1798 in a positive spirit of reconciliation, and in cooperation with many voluntary organisations, North and South, without seeking to gloss over difficult issues or unpalatable realities. Our objective should be a deeper understanding of what happened, so that we can draw from it inspiration and instruction for our own time, as well as show respect for our forebears who suffered at the time, not any superficial or revisionist exercise.

The 1790s is arguably a pivotal decade in the evolution of modern Ireland. It witnessed the emergence of popular Republicanism and Loyalism, of separatism, of the Orange Order and Maynooth College, and culminated in the 1798 Rebellion and the Act of Union of 1800, which defined subsequent relations between Ireland and Britain. The decade presents an interesting interplay between Irish and international forces, when what happened on the island was inseparable from a wider global setting. It was one of many occasions, when a selfish strategic interest prevailed over the rights of the people.

1798 also cast a long shadow. The resonant and romantic names of Theobald Wolfe Tone, Henry Joy McCracken, Beauchamp Bagenal Harvey, Thomas Russell, Robert Emmett, Lord Edward Fitzgerald, Father John Murphy and Miles Byme, amongst many others, were to reverberate down the echo chambers of Irish history. While physically defeated, they achieved a remarkable symbolic victory, which has ensured their undying fame.

If the 1790s can be seen as the pivotal decade in the evolution of modern Ireland, then an honest and accurate understanding of it is not just of historical interest, but has important implications for current political and cultural thinking. It is precisely because of its enduring relevance that 1798 has never entirely passed out of politics and into history. A window of opportunity was opened in Ireland by the impact of the American and French Revolutions; that moment was brilliantly seized by the United Irishmen who imaginatively created a vision of a non-sectarian, democratic and inclusive politics, which could attract and sustain all Irish people in all their inherited complexities.

Rather than seeing religious, ethnic and political diversity as a disabling problem, the United Irishmen saw it as a glorious opportunity to construct a wider, more tolerant and generous vision of Irish identity. Rather than grimly clinging to a divisive past, the United Irishmen sought to create a shared future. In their first declaration of principle, they stated:

> In thus associating, we have thought little about our ancestors, much about our posterity. Are we forever to walk like beasts of prey over the fields which these ancestors stained with blood?

That remains just as true after another 200 years.

Myles Byrne rejected again and again in his memoirs the attempt to depict 1798 as a religious war-cum-peasants-revolt, when its object was "to obtain equal and adequate rights for people of every religious persuasion, and for the complete independence of their country". In reply to the distinguished author Gustave de Beaumont, in 1840, he listed "the many distinguished Irish Protestants" as well as Catholics "who sacrificed their lives and fortunes in the cause of the independence of their country."

The United Irishmen were for bringing the ideals of the American Declaration of Independence, the French Declaration of the Rights of Man, the doctrines of Rousseau and Tom Paine, to bear on the Irish situation. France, through the Revolution, had shown to all that liberty was possible in a predominantly Catholic country. The United Irishmen were treated as dangerous democrats - democrat being then a word of abuse with subversive connotations. The opposing ideal was 'our glorious Constitution', as apologists for the existing order of king, lords and commons put it, with the insufferable smugness and self satisfaction that has sometimes tended to surround the worship of British institutions. Nicholas Furlong cites the example of the landlord Lord Mountnorris addressing Father John Murphy's unimpressed congregation at Boolavogue, urging them to give up their makeshift weapons. (The sequel, when those who did became marked men in the eyes of the authorities, is an illustration of all the historical problems surrounding the issue of decommissioning). The 'glorious Constitution' consisted of narrow oligarchy, propped up by rotten and pocket boroughs and persistent sectarian domination and wholesale corruption within a system that was representative in appearance only.

When Lord Fitzwilliam tried to introduce what we might nowadays call 'confidence-building measures', in terms of removing remaining Catholic disabilities and tried to dismiss the old guard, he was peremptorily recalled. A telling commentary was that the Government of William Pitt in London sided with the French *emigrés* and the ousted *Ancien Régime* in France, with which the 'glorious Constitution' had apparently more in common by the 1790s, than with the democratic ideals of America and France. The provoking and the suppression of the 1798 rebellion was about the putting down of democracy in Ireland for a long time to come, whether in terms of parliamentary reform, Catholic emancipation or national independence, and the establishment of a Union in perpetuity, which would hopefully ensure that the Catholic majority in Ireland would always be an impotent political minority, even in the event of later reform and emancipation.

The political architecture of these islands is built partly on the Act of Union as a foundation, while the 1790s demonstrate the difficulties in creating a politics capable of representing all of the Irish people and their inherited complexities, and of solving the perplexing 'Rubik's cube' of nation, Church, State, empire and class. The 1790s force us to confront these thorny issues, rather than naively wishing for their easy reconciliation or transcendence.

Many of the Ulster Presbyterian members of the United Irishmen would have been heavily influenced, as were the American revolutionaries of that era, by the greatest Irish political philosopher of that, or indeed any other time, Francis Hutcheson, who taught in Dublin and in Glasgow University. Hutcheson insisted on the accountability of rulers to the people, who had the right to replace them. He believed the best State was a small Republic, where people and governors would be close to each other, and it was his view that if upon any trial the people find that the plan of power they constituted avowedly for their own good is really dangerous to them, they have a right to alter it. It must be strange effrontery in any governor ... to hold them to a contract which he previously entered into for this expectation and express sign that it should tend to the general good, for which also he expressly undertook, when it is found to have a contrary tendency.

In an eerie way, the problems of the 1790s are still with us today, 200 years later. Like the Fall of the Bastille, the Fall of the Berlin Wall signalled the collapse of old certainties at the beginning of this decade. But as in the 1790s, the outcome of what had seemed to be an event ushering in a glorious new European epoch of peaceful revolutions was uncertainty and, eventually, European conflict in certain areas. The 1790s saw the horrendous struggle between France and England, the reign of Terror, and the savagery of the *Vendée*.

The 1990s have equally seen, not only the dawning of a new age of freedom, but the grotesque horrors of Bosnia. Equally, in Ireland the 1790s opened with a glorious, optimistic sense of sweeping political change leading to a brighter future and hopes which were to be cruelly dashed. In the 1990s, peace processes began in many conflicts in a similar warm glow of optimism. Some have succeeded, as in South Africa, while others, such as the Middle East, are in severe difficulties.

There are, therefore, instructive parallels between the two end of century decades, at both the European and the Irish level. Given the delicate state of the Peace Process we need to learn all the lessons that Irish history can teach us - and the the period of the 1790s is particularly instructive.

One lesson we particularly need to pay heed to is the divisive role of propaganda and selective history. The propaganda war during and after 1798 ensured that the real principles of the 1790s were buried in a welter of recrimination and attempted political vindication. The propaganda war also aggravated the fear and the subsequent violence. The more unsympathetic members of the Ascendancy party regarded the Irish, like the Boers regarded the Hottentots, as not entitled to civilised treatment and as barbarians intent on massacre. One judge, Lord Clonmell, explicitly used the Southern African comparison.

On the other hand, the United Irishmen tried to mobilise maximum political support by depicting all their opponents as merciless Orangemen intent on extermination. In the acrimonious and anxious aftermath of 1798 and the Act of Union, control of the interpretation of the Rebellion became a vital component of many political agendas. Considerable energy was invested in portraying the 1798 Rebellion as mere sectarian and agrarian Popular revolt, in a largely successful effort to detach and turn away middle class Northern Presbyterians from their Republican ideas and from the emerging democratic movement.

Recent work on the period has begun to make 1798 available in a fresh way, opening a more generous space in which to consider and debate it. There is of course no one 'right' interpretation of 1798, which had short-term, medium-term and long-term effects, all of which can be properly argued over. But there is no doubt that we need to cast our net more widely, and go beyond the previously dominant emphasis on the sectarian version of '98, derived in part from a polemical post-rebellion falsification propagated by people totally opposed to Catholic Emancipation, and who thought the only thing wrong with the Penal Laws was the feeble execution of them. We must do that without denying that sectarian outrages and murders, or what Wolfe Tone called "a system of assassination", did occur on both sides, or that acute sectarian fears and feelings ran high.

Lecky quotes the relatively humane Viceroy Lord Cornwallis as expressing indignation at the folly of substituting the word Catholicism instead of Jacobinism as the foundation of the rebellion:

> The violence of our friends and their folly in endeavouring to make it
> a religious war added to the ferocity of your troops, who delight in
> murder, most powerfully counteract all plans of conciliation.

Bishop Stock of Killala, later Bishop of Waterford, deeply regretted that the Orange Society had ever appeared "to furnish the Romanists too plausible a pretext for alarm and hostility against their Protestant brethren", illustrating the truth seen in our own day that abuse of majority power in one area can unjustly redound to the disadvantage of the same community where it is a minority elsewhere. A sensitive memorial is planned by Wexford County Council for Scullabogue in

Wexford, for example, but there is also a need to acknowledge the appalling acts of repression by the authorities, in the same way that regret has been expressed for the Famine. In 1813 William Sampson, a Protestant United Irish lawyer, told a New York courtroom

> that government that refused to tolerate Catholics, tolerated, instigated and indemnified a faction whose deeds will never be forgotten ... then it was, that a spectacle, new and appalling, for the first time presented itself, and Presbyterian, Churchman and Catholic were seen to ascend the same scaffold, and die in the cause of an indissoluble union.

As a result Mayor Clinton of New York, by no means the last of his name to be moved in an Irish cause, upheld, in a landmark case, the freedom and confidentiality of the Catholic confessional.

The single most important determinant of the 1798 Rebellion was mass-politicisation in the 1790s. The mainly middle class United Irishmen joined forces with the people organised in the Defenders, who were especially strong in what later became the border areas. Sometimes, to make a political point in our own day, the positive ideals of the United Irishmen have been contrasted with the more one dimensional popular goals and objectives of the Defenders. The reality of Irish nationalism through history is that lofty and tolerant ideals uniting the traditions have always needed to seek popular support, in the main only available from the tradition of the majority. It was politicisation which created the explosive cocktail of political, social, religious and economic forces in the area. The reception of the ideology of revolutionary France was crucial; its primary impact was to widen and deepen pre-existing divisions within Irish political culture, between reformist and conservative elements, pushing one towards radicalism and the other towards repression, as the 1790s progressed.

These new interpretations and vistas need to be incorporated into the commemoration of the Bicentenary of the Rebellion. '98 does not belong exclusively to any one political tradition in Ireland.

The Catholic-Nationalist version of '98 - which dominated the 1898, 1938 and 1948 Commemorations - needs to be enlarged in favour of greater emphasis on a pluralist, non-sectarian approach, which more accurately reflects what the United Irishmen originally envisaged. Seán Lemass, when he was Taoiseach, said, referring to the situation up to the 1960s, that it might be better if in some of our educational establishments "Wolfe Tone's conception of the Irish nation was better understood and respected." (From John Horgan's recent biography)

If we are fully to re-engage with the invigorating vision of the United Irishmen, we must avoid too much exclusive concentration of a vivid imagination on the purely military aspects of 1798, with pikes and deaths, murder and martyrdom, while retaining respect for the dead and for the mass of people, some of whom were to suffer appalling repression. We should put the emphasis today on the living principles of democracy and pluralism which the United Irishmen so nobly formulated. The details of the military campaign, which are understandably of absorbing interest to many people with roots and ancestors in the areas concerned, should not distract us from the enduring legacy of the political vision and moral choices which impelled men and women into the field in 1798. It is that political vision we need to reclaim and remember, rather than the physical defeat of the revolution on the bloody battlefields of '98.

We need to adhere to the international perspective of the United Irishmen - to link Bunker Hill, the Bastille and Boolavogue, to stress the enduring links which '98 forged with America, France and Australia. 1798 in Wexford was not just a number of minor skirmishes, but part of a national and indeed international campaign, indelibly linked to what had been happening elsewhere - an Irish echo of the distant drums of the Atlantic Revolution. It was Ireland's first modern revolution. Citizen Edward Fitzgerald, sometime inhabitant of Leinster House; Wolfe Tone; Robert Emmett and many others among the leaders, had a hardened revolutionary purpose. Unfortunately for them, things did not come together at the right time. A successful revolution had to wait another 120 years. Anyone who thinks that a form of rule devised in the twin interests of a monopolistic Ascendancy and the protection of a neighbouring country were likely to be peacefully dismantled without a struggle is doing little justice to the ruthless determination which opposed Irish freedom, in even its mildest forms, for so long.

In response to this global dimension, our commemoration needs to be international and national as well as local. In particular, we must be generous in our acknowledgement of the Ulster dimension and especially of the major contribution of the Presbyterian tradition at that time, with its enlightened emphasis on justice, equality and liberty.

We can make the United Irish speak to the Irish people as a whole, including the *diaspora*. We can use the 1790s as a lesson and an inspiration for the 1990s. Wolfe Tone has not been proved wrong in his assertion that to achieve the aspect of asserting the independence of his country it was necessary to unite at least some of the different traditions. On that front he achieved more than any of us have done since his time.

Many of the Presbyterian United Irish Leaders of the North understood the need for equality and inclusion. They and their generosity of spirit remain to this day an honour to the tradition from which they came. They realised, sooner than most, that 'Croppies lie down', or as people would say today 'lower your expectations' was not a viable policy for the long run, and that it would damage what they wanted for themselves. The right to participate in an inclusive national democracy and in national political life is as valid an objective today as it was 200 years ago. Today, the real test is to hold united to an intelligent political strategy without reversion to violence.

Only recently, have historians begun to recover the buried history of the embryonic Wexford Republic of June 1798, the Senate of which contained equal numbers of Protestants and Catholics and which is an important symbol of the spirit of the Commemoration. With the defeat of the United Irish, this innovative experiment in democracy was suppressed with great brutality and obliterated from the historical record; its widespread support at all levels of Wexford society was denied in the anxious aftermath of 1798, and the revolution itself was then dismissively misrepresented.

By recovering the real history of the Wexford Republic, we are reappropriating a profoundly democratic symbol, and an inspiring example of an embryonic effort to construct a representative, secular and pluralist politics on the island of Ireland. 200 years later, it can again serve to encourage us towards that imaginative inclusiveness which the United Irish had identified as being essential to unite Protestant, Catholic and Dissenter.

Half a century later in the 1840s, at the time of Young Ireland and the ballad *Who fears to speak of '98?* and also of RR Madden's memoirs on the lives of the leaders of the Rebellion, the thread was picked up again, evidenced by the cultural nationalism preached by Thomas Davis. In the 1790s this had only begun to germinate, in

Edward Bunting's *Irish Airs*, in which Thomas Russell, the first Linenhall Librarian, took a keen interest.

It is wrong to think that any previous generation had all the answers, or that they are to be found solely in one tradition. If they had or were, it would be unlikely we would have the difficulties that we still experience today. As we should be warned from many periods of our history, what may seem like brilliant opportunities can disappear with frightening speed, in many cases never to be recovered within a lifetime. The human tragedy involved was expressed by William Drennan in a verse in 1806 :

INDEPENDENCE shot past him in letters of light,
Then the scroll seemed to shrivel, and vanish in night;
And all the illumin'd horizon became,
In the shift of a moment, a darkness - a dream

We need to understand the reasons for the parting of the ways after 1798, how most of the Protestant radicals and their descendants came eventually to be supporters of the Union and in many cases allies of their earlier opponents the Orangemen, although threads of the radical Presbyterian tradition survived to the Home Rule controversies and even to this day. It would be wrong to think that the United Irishmen belong exclusively to our present-day Nationalist tradition. They belong equally to the beginnings of a democratic tradition, which can be shared by all. Unionists and especially Presbyterians are entitled and should be encouraged to see in them part of their own traditions. The Protestant churches collectively might acknowledge more freely the formative role that some of their number working with their leading Catholic contemporaries played in paving the way for the independent Ireland we have today.

Speaking personally, I would like to see the Church leaders acknowledge clearly that this State today in no way threatens, either inside or outside its jurisdiction, any sane conception of the Protestant identity, and on the contrary is supportive of it in many different ways, as it is of other mainstream religious professions. In Northern Ireland itself, and not for any outside reason, it is the pockets of hardcore bigotry and sectarianism that belong to a bygone age and are under serious threat from modern civilisation, including modern Christian thinking. The sort of attitude that lumps Ecumenism, Romanism, Nationalism and Republicanism as related enemies all in the one basket would have been very reactionary paranoia even in the 1790s and has no future in a modern Britain, let alone a modern Ireland. Civil and religious liberty were conspicuous by their absence in the Ireland of the Penal Laws. It was not till 1791, when the Society of United Irishmen was founded, that the real struggle for them began. They wanted to substitute the Fourteenth of July for the Twelfth, as the day of celebration and as a more appropriate foundation day.

Commemorations are occasions to be handled sensitively. They revive old memories and frequently mixed feelings. The bicentenary of 1798 affords no occasion for triumphalism on any side. It represented the defeat of ideals capable of bringing peace, democracy and justice early to Ireland, and for a long time an end to hopes of a viable independence, initially under French protection. People were crushed, but the ideals lived on. The challenge that has faced every succeeding generation is how to translate these ideals into reality. The periodic conflict since 1798 over a 300 year cycle, and the development of very entrenched political differences over the past 100 years or more, has made this immensely difficult today. But we have to keep striving, till we succeed. The traditions have to be encouraged to come together and to find some form of agreement and accommodation. That necessity is recognised on all sides.

The projected form of union between Irishmen in the 1790s did not work or last. We will have to find one that will, free of illusion, but not of generosity. ●

The Politics of Memory

The Contemporary Significance of the 1798 Rebellion

by Kevin Whelan

"... it was proposed to me that I should help my downtrodden countrymen by assembling with other Irishmen to romance about 1798. Until Irishmen apply themselves to what the condition of Ireland will be in 1998 they will get very little patriotism out of Yours sincerely."
George Bernard Shaw (1898)

Kevin Whelan is a historical geographer and Dublin Director of Notre Dame University. He has published numerous articles on 1798.

143

Introduction

The 1790s was an extraordinary decade in Irish history, when the opportunity presented itself to transcend the age-old sectarian, ethnic and political divisions of the island. The United Irish movement had, as its central aim, the demolition of a political system rooted in sectarian privilege and its replacement with a secular democratic politics, founded on universal ideas of equality and justice. The project of creating a secular republic, recasting political participation on inclusive lines, was deliberately blocked by the British state, using the weapons of sectarianism, military terror in 1798 and the suppression of the Irish parliament. We are still living with the consequences of that defeat. Two centuries later, after the loss of the one realistic opportunity Ireland has had to benefit from the advances of the European Enlightenment, the sectarian alternative forced upon it in the crucial decade of the 1790s still survives, as a distorting feature of British-Irish and internal Irish relations. Witness the last three years at Drumcree - archaic images broadcast to a world at once horrified and fascinated by them.

With the blockage of the United Irish project, Irish politics split into two fragments - nationalism and unionism - which still dominate the political landscape two centuries later. Like the United Irishmen, we face the task today of negotiating an agreed political structure, capable of representing Irish people in all their inherited complexities. Unless we understand the reason for the defeat of the United Irish project in the 1790s, we are poorly equipped to avoid a lethal repetition.

While at one level 1798 is about history, at another it is equally about the present. By showing how much political orientations have changed since the 1790s, we can see that political positions in the North are not in any sense set in stone. If things have changed so much in the past they can do so again in the future.

If the 1790s can be seen as the pivotal decade in the evolution of modern Ireland, then an honest and accurate understanding of it is not just of scholarly interest, but has important implications for current political and cultural thinking. It is precisely because of its enduring relevance that 1798 has never truly passed out of politics and into history. The United Irishmen's ideas did not die with the events, but are still potent, valid and unrealised. In the sense that they faced the same problems which bedevil modern Ireland, the United Irishmen are very much our contemporaries.

We need to stress their enduring legacy - the political vision and moral choices which impelled men and women into the field in 1798. It is this political vision that we must reclaim, not the physical defeat of the revolution on the bloody battlefields of '98. As Milan Kundera has noted, "the struggle for power is the struggle of memory against forgetting". In the case of 1798 it is not what we remember that is the problem, but what we have forgotten.

The French Revolution

The French Revolution made buoyant the weight of history - the dead hand of the dead generations, weighing like a nightmare on the brains of the living, where the political world appeared as an immutable force, pressing down relentlessly on the self. By making hope and history rhyme, the French Revolution freed political desire, desire in the Lacanian sense, as the locus of change and the movement of freedom. Releasing this frozen desire into the living stream of history also freed the utopian political instinct to educate that desire and to direct its trajectory.

The French Revolution's promotion of human rights offered an alternative path to the idea of a political community. The universality of the Republican principles of *'liberté, egalité, fraternité'* provided a neutral language with which to consider the characteristics of a just State. This universality supplied an alternative basis for uniting disparate peoples, generating the possibility of a common political home, based on transparent compliance with ethical rather than ethnic principles, on justice, not 'history'. As we stand on the cusp of the third millennium, these principles retain their potency.

A window of opportunity was opened in Ireland by the impact of the American and French Revolutions: that moment was brilliantly seized by the United Irishmen, who imaginatively created a vision of a non-sectarian, democratic and inclusive politics, which could attract and sustain all Irish people in all their inherited complexities. Rather than seeing religious, ethnic and political diversity as a disabling problem the United Irishmen saw it as a glorious opportunity to construct a wider, more tolerant and generous vision of Irish identity. Rather than clinging grimly to a divided and divisive past, a stifling sepulchre of precedents, the United Irishmen sought to create a shared future, a cradle of possibilities.

By facing into the future rather than the past they wished to heal the hurts of Irish history in a brotherhood of affection. In their first declaration of principle they stated:

> We have thought much about our posterity, little about our ancestors. Are we forever to walk like beasts of prey over the fields which these ancestors stained with blood?

We cannot overemphasise the United Irish emphasis on being in the European vanguard, of facing the future, not the past. Their political necks were set in concrete, facing relentlessly forward. It was as if they wished to reorient Walter Benjamin's 'Angel of History' - to swivel it away from the desolate debris of the past and to face it into the empty and therefor endless possibilities of the future:

> A Klee painting named *Angelus Novus* shows an angel looking as though he is about to move away from something he is fixedly contemplating. His eyes are staring, his mouth is open, his wings are spread. This is how one pictures the angel of history. His face is turned toward the past. Where we perceive a chain of events, he sees one single catastrophe which keeps piling wreckage upon wreckage and hurls it in front of his feet. The angel would like to stay, awaken the dead, and make whole what has been smashed. But a storm is blowing from Paradise; it has got caught in his wings with such violence that the angel can no longer close them. This storm irresistibly propels him into the future to which his back is turned, while the pile of debris before him grows skyward. This storm is what we call progress.

As the American novelist Herman Melville claimed, "The past is the textbook of tyrants: the future is the Bible of the free."

Tone's *Argument on behalf of the Catholics of Ireland* broke the sectarian mould of Irish politics. Along with Russell, Neilson and Drennan, he proposed the creation of the United Irishmen with a political project of common citizenship and parity of esteem for the main traditions of Ireland. Tone was later to describe his aim in a memorable aphorism: "to substitute the common name of Irishman in

place of the denominations of Protestants, Catholics and Dissenters."
Fired by French ideals during the heady days of the early 1790s when
it seemed that Enlightenment principles would receive universal
political expression, the United Irishmen were established in a blaze of
optimism, in Belfast and Dublin in 1791.

The Novelty of the United Irishmen

The United Irishmen were therefore heirs to three revolutions, but they
were not merely copycat importers. As they themselves stated, in their
Address to Scottish Radicals in 1993:

> We will not buy nor borrow liberty from American,
> nor from France, but we will manufacture it ourselves
> and work it up with those materials which the hearts
> of Irishmen furnish them with at home

There were three novel elements to the United Irish project.

Catholics as Citizens

As articulated by Theobald Wolfe Tone, the United Irishmen
audaciously expanded the doctrinaire Whig version of liberty to
include Catholics. They thus secularised liberty, in a way free of either
the sectarian exclusions of the English Revolution and of the atheistic
and anti-traditional thrust of the French Revolution. This expansion of
the polity to include Catholics exposed the limits of Britishness and
focused its scrutiny more obsessively on Ireland, hitherto a colony run
by remote control. Ireland and America were at the inner and the outer
periphery of the 18th century British Empire.

With the outer periphery detaching itself, Britain was determined not
to allow the strategically much more important inner periphery of
Ireland to follow suit. Britain's self interest was such that it was unable
to countenance an independent Ireland and its imagined community
was also so narrowly envisioned as to be incapable of absorbing
Catholics as citizens. That imaginative and political failure of
Britishness was to be at the heart of the Anglo-Irish problem in the
1790s: its effects can be seen ever more clearly as the concept of
Britishness decomposes in the 1990s.

It is increasingly apparent that the arc of Empire and the arc of Britishness were directly synchronous. With Empire gone, with Protestantism fading in the face of a secularising and multi-cultural society, and with its old continental adversaries now its partners in the EU, Britishness no longer has a coherent principle. Recent developments in Scotland and Wales indicate the new realities, while in a sense returning to pre-imperial and pre-Union politics. These developments have also striking implications for Northern Ireland, which are slowly surfacing in the political arena. In this startling rupture, the United Irishmen broke with the sedimented anti-popery of the English Whigs, and thereby shattered the sectarian moulds of the Irish 18th century.

Separatism

A second innovation in United Irish thinking was its espousal of separatism. They believed that the sectarian Irish state (symbolised by its unreformed parliament) was underpinned by the British connection. Remove that connection and it would collapse. Wolfe Tone wrote that:

> The influence of England was the radical vice of our government and consequently Ireland would never be free, prosperous or happy until she was independent. And that independence was unattainable while the connection which England existed.

By contrast, and illustrating the novelty of the Irish Enlightenment, the Scottish Enlightenment was conceived and developed as a unionist project which increased the integration between Scotland and England in a shared Britishness. Just as it proved incapable of absorbing Catholicism, Britishness proved equally incapable of ingesting Irishness (as it had absorbed Welshness and Scottishness). By offering a political analysis of this failure, the United Irishmen explicitly brought separatism onto the Irish political agenda for the first time.

Vernacular Visions

In terms of cultural politics the United Irishmen disputed the standard Enlightenment espousal of universalism and rejection of regional cultures as inevitably doomed to obsolescence. They argued instead for an equal weighting of cultures (parity of esteem), signified in the Irish case by giving proper weight to the Gaelic (indigenous) elements. By retrieving and then returning the native to the high cultural ground, the United Irishmen espoused an exemplary cultural pluralism of a most radical kind. They sought to deepen the timeline of Irish history to include the despised pre-colonial past, but not to claim that past as the exclusive preserve of the indigenous Irish, but as a shared and valued birthright of all Irish people. By imagining this inclusive Irish past, the United Irishmen also rejected the exclusive British past in Ireland as a divisive colonial hangover. The United Irishmen

were, therefore, bearers of an alternative Enlightenment, which respected cultural specificity and balanced the rights of man (individual and inalienable) with the rights of cultures, however small, to self-respect and self-determination. In this sense, the United Irishmen were not cultural but republican nationalists.

The celebrated Belfast Harp Festival, held in 1792, was a public expression of this new determination to give equal weight to the Gaelic as well as the English component in Irish culture. The United Irishmen, notably Sampson, Russell and MacNeven, saw the need to balance the particularity of national culture alongside the universal and cosmopolitan political ideals of the Enlightenment. The Harp Festival was a public gesture in this direction. Just as in the religious sphere, the United Irishmen sought to move beyond the disabling binaries of 'colonial' and 'native' and to assert the shared ownership of a rich Irish past by all the traditions of Ireland.

The United Irishmen's miscellany *Bolg an tSolair* (1795) was a similar assertion of cultural appropriation, as was their adoption of the slogan *Éireann go brách* (Ireland Forever), their use of popular Gaelic tunes for their political ballads and their encouragement of the cult of Carolan as the national bard. These initiatives deepened the politics of culture which had emerged in the 1780s, most notably in the innovative volumes of Charlotte Brooke and JC Walker and in the powerfully expressed nationalism of the Volunteer movement.

The Defeat of the United Irishmen

By the early 1790s, it was becoming increasingly clear that the French Revolution would unleash a titanic European struggle between 'democracy' and 'aristocracy', between Republicanism and monarchy, between *liberté, egalité* and *fraternité*' and the *ancien régime*. Burke's emotional tirade, *Reflections on the Revolution in France* and Paine's caustic republican response, *The Rights of Man,* established the battlefield as one of ideas. As France and Great Britain moved inexorably towards conflict, it became apparent that this would be the first modern war, a new war of principle and ideology rather than an old war of tactical and dynastic advantage. The French mass mobilisation of highly motivated citizen-soldiers as opposed to reliance on a small professional standing army redefined the very nature of warfare. The number of combatants and casualties escalated to unheard-of proportions, and the theatre of war aggressively expanded to embrace all Europe.

In these circumstances, once war formally broke out in 1793, the United Irishmen, grudgingly tolerated in peace-time, were immediately banned as a potentially (if not actually) treasonable organisation. Concessions to Catholics, granted both to keep them from the clutches of the United Irishmen and to trade relief for recruits, stopped. An increasingly rigid conservative regime under William Pitt took over in Britain, a regime which instinctively sided with the *Ancien Régime in France,* thereby demonstrating the shallowness of the democratic credentials of the Glorious Revolution. As the French Revolution degenerated into the Terror and as France itself showed signs of sweeping across Europe not as a new army of liberation but as an old despotic conqueror, the radical enthusiasm of the 1790s sobered into a more pragmatic political assessment. Faced with state repression, the United Irishmen faced the options of shutting up or putting up.

The recall of Fitzwilliam as Lord-Lieutenant in 1795 marked a turning point. A Burkean Whig, Fitzwilliam had come to Ireland determined to grant Catholic Emancipation, to face down Beresford, Fitzgibbon and Foster, and to promote Irish Whigs like Henry Grattan. When he quickly put this programme into operation, Prime Minister William Pitt sacked him, dashing Catholic hopes of full emancipation and marking an end to legislative concessions to the radicals. After Fitzwilliam, Catholic activists showed a new willingness to join the United Irishmen. Their leader, John Keogh stated bluntly: "There is no longer a Catholic question: there is only the Irish question", while Bishop Thomas Hussey believed that the recall of Fitzwilliam left Ireland "on the brink of civil war".

The 1790s was a pivotal decade in modern European history. England and France were locked into an international battle for domination, in the first great war in which modernity confronted tradition. The loaded meanings of these two words were to be increased and diversified endlessly throughout their epic contest. In Ireland the United Irishmen - and with them political modernity - were its casualties. The United Irish project was defeated by the London and Dublin governments, who deliberately injected sectarianism as an antidote to them. The Orange Order was used as an instrument of policy - but carefully cloaked as an ostensibly spontaneous combustion of 'vulgar loyalism' - an uncontainable surge of legitimate Protestant anxieties and anger at the assault made on its alleged 'civil liberties'.

An equally crucial sectarian card was the institutional Catholic church, recruited to the standard of loyalism as a joint victim (with the British state) of the French secular and Republican project, and appeased by the British through state funding of a national Catholic seminary at Maynooth. These 'twin peaks' of sectarianism - the Orange Order and Maynooth College - were both institutionalised at precisely the same moment in 1795 as counter-revolutionary bulwarks against the non-sectarian revolution of the United Irishmen, which was seen as triply threatening: to the Irish state; the British system; and the Catholic church.

After mid 1795 the United Irish merger with the Defenders proceeded apace. From the conservative perspective this created the nightmare security scenario of the United Irishmen overrunning all of Ulster and controlling the island north of a line from Dundalk to Sligo.

In this context the crucial buffer zone was in the Lough Neagh crescent, running from Dungannon to Lisburn, and centered in the cockpit of north Armagh. If the United Irishmen could spread unhindered down the Lagan valley, across north Armagh and into the Defender country of south Ulster, the north would be effectively lost. The founding of the Orange Order (the 'vulgar conservative' equivalent of the Church and King mobs in England, with a vitriolic sectarian tinge) and the 'Armagh expulsions' of late 1795, made sense in this context.

The Orange Order was established in north Armagh, discreetly backed by local gentry and generals, to stiffen the loyalist backbone and drive an Anglican wedge between Presbyterian/United Irish Antrim and Down, and Catholic/Defender south Ulster. The non-sectarian appeal of the United Irishmen was now being met by a resoundingly sectarian Orange stance - which emphasised Englishness not Irishness, the past not the future, and disunited rather than united Irishmen.

The 'Armagh expulsions' of 1795-6 involved sectarian assaults on Catholic homes in mid-Ulster, under the threat of being sent to 'Hell or Connaught'. 5,000 Catholics were forced out, mostly moving to Mayo and Galway, but also scattering to Belfast (where they were sheltered by the United Irishmen), to Drogheda and to Dublin, to Scotland and to America. There was a close correlation between the scene of the expulsions and the spread of the Orange Order. While publicly disapproving, Dublin Castle, briefed by local loyalists and generals, refused to intervene. This period marked the first deployment of raw sectarianism as a counter-revolutionary measure by the state.

As a direct consequence, revived sectarian animosity infected a barren political landscape that came to look increasingly anachronistic and increasingly 'Irish'. The only way that the Irish could be safely accommodated within the Union was to be demodernised politically and then have these anachronisms ascribed to their native backwardness, rather than to a toxic policy of sectarianism, military coercion and cultural regression.

In this respect, it became vitally important to see 1798 not as an attempt to overthrow reaction and replace it with enlightenment, but as a rehearsal of the old sectarian animosities, cunningly disguised in a new political and French vocabulary. European history might be transformed, but Irish history was doomed to inexorably reproduce the monotonous pattern of the past.

What happened after '98 is equally important to what happened during it. The rebellion immediately became a political football, endlessly kicked about during the interminable Union debates. Writing in the shadow of that debate, early commentators were either pro or anti-Union. If pro-Union they tended to soft pedal on the issue of Catholic and United Irish culpability for the rebellion, stressing instead the provocation of the loyalists and the Orange Order. Anti-Unionists (the die hard loyalist faction) stressed instead the 'popish plot' interpretation, seeing the rebellion as the third in the trinity of 1641, 1690 and 1798.

The propaganda war which ensued after 1798 ensured that the real principles of the 1790s were buried in a welter of recrimination and political point-scoring. In the acrimonious and anxious aftermath of 1798 and the Act of Union, control of the interpretation of the rebellion became a vital component of many political agendas. Considerable energy was invested in portraying the 1798 rebellion as a mere sectarian and agrarian revolt of ignorant catholic peasants, in an effort to detach Presbyterians from the emerging democratic movement. This viewpoint is essentially a product of post-Rebellion propaganda, which suited both the government (anxious to diminish the threat of radical politics and to detach the Ulster Presbyterians from their anti-establishment stance), and the United Irishmen (who were keen to distance themselves from the culpability for organising a bloody armed insurrection).

The Presbyterian radical James Hope later commented on the extent of these distortions, even by former colleagues:

> It is hard for a man who did not live at the time, to believe or comprehend the extent to which misrepresentations were carried at the close of our struggle; for, besides the paid agents, the men who flinched and fell away from our cause, grasped at any apology for their own delinquency.

By bitter experience Hope understood the import of the proverb 'victory has a thousand fathers but defeat is an orphan', or the bitter aphorism of the French revolutionary St Just: "They who make half-revolutions dig their own graves".

153

The Politics of Memory

Almost as they were happening, the events of 1798 were being recast in terms of memory. As with the politics, the memory also split into two fragments. In the Unionist one, 1798 was figured as a sectarian blood bath, yet another chapter in the Protestant Book of Martyrs. In the Catholic Nationalist one, 1798 became a struggle for faith and fatherland, in which the United Irishmen and Presbyterians were airbrushed out of a picture increasingly dominated by the clerical collar of 'Father Murphy'. This partisan confiscation of the memory of 1798 by the Catholics erased a distinguished moment in the history of Ulster Presbyterianism. Today the global image of Ulster Protestants is dominated by the apocalyptic footage from places like Drumcree and they are often presented as reactionaries, lost in the mists of sectarian bigotry.

Yet in the 1790s, Belfast, the 'Athens of the North', was the birthplace of Irish separatism and the cradle of the United Irish movement. The Ulster Presbyterians were at the cutting edge of the emerging radical movement and provided many of its most talented leaders. Their generosity of spirit, political vision, imaginative inclusiveness and commitment to the principles of justice remain to this day an honour to the tradition from which they sprang, even thought this distinguished period in their evolution does not figure prominently in their current self-image. Flickering hesitantly behind the obscuring smoke of the 'Twelfth' there is another, more generous history of Ulster Presbyterianism, of which they are aware, but wary.

While the past cannot be restored, memory can. We need a process of rememoration - a retrieving of memory which had been deliberately suppressed. Restoring this enabling memory can help release the blockage: the endless calendrical cycle of Protestant memory - the mythic circle of repetition can be redirected into historical and linear time, in which the possibility of progress finally becomes available. By elevating politics out of the sectarian rut in which it has been deliberately confined since 1798, the dead weight of the continuous past can be lifted and political buoyancy restored. The power of political memory, which links past and present dynamically, needs to be a central interpretive focus in any understanding of 1798.

The Presbyterian Withdrawal

After '98, the government moved rapidly to restore the Presbyterians to the Protestant and conservative consensus. As Alexander Knox reported to Castlereagh on 15th July 1803:

> This is perhaps a more favourable moment for forming a salutary connection between government and the Presbyterian body of Ulster than any that may again arrive. The republicanism of that part of Ireland is checked and repressed by the cruelties of Roman Catholics in the late rebellion, and by the despotism of Bonaparte. They are, therefore, in a humour for acquiescing in the views of government beyond what they were, or (should the opportunity be missed) may be hereafter. How much then, is it to be wished that, while the tide of their wrong passions is so unusually low, a mound should be raised that will for ever after be a safe restraint to them.

Thus religious and political conflict ultimately underwrote rather than undermined Protestant religious allegiance in Ulster. A popular Protestant identity transcending its confessional variety could then emerge, consolidating around shared opposition to the Catholic claims and nationalist ones, once Catholicism usurped that name, a process accelerated by O'Connell's explicitly sectarian politics.

The Irish window of opportunity opened by the French Revolution was forcibly closed. In the aftermath of 1798 and its rancorous polemics which peddled sectarian glosses, and given the changing international fortunes of 'popery' after Napoleon's *concordat* with the Pope ("the dog returning to its own vomit," as William Wordsworth described it), the United Irish movement passed and croppies were forced to lie down.

The revived sectarian divides in Ulster greatly suited the British government. The Chief Secretary Sir Robert Peel would write in 1813: "the government could scarcely wish to see the lower classes in the north of Ireland united". He hoped they would always be disunited: "The great art is to keep them so, and yet at peace or rather not at war with each other."

And so the Presbyterians were encouraged to forget their distinguished contribution to the United Irish movement. By 1844 a Belfast chapbook history of the rebellion could note:

155

Since, from the experience of the event, civil war in any part of Ireland, except some northern counties, must from whatever cause excited, be justly expected to assume a religious complexion of the most bloody hue, Irish Protestants ought to be convinced that the political separation of their country from Britain by a popular insurrection must involve their extinction and that consequently an infrangibly determined adherence to their British connection is necessary for their safety.

The long-term import of their withdrawal from radicalism was to leave Presbyterians both intellectually and politically comatose. The bifurcation into nationalist and unionist led to a shrivelling of political debate and the obsessive nationalist concern with '98 in the 19th century was met on the unionist side by a contrapuntal strategy of deliberate amnesia.

The Catholic Version of 1798

In the immediate and bloody aftermath of 1798, the United Irishmen kept a low profile. In a damage-limitation exercise, the less radical wing of the United Irishmen played down their role in organising the rebellion (as in the evasive, apologetic accounts of Edward Hay, Thomas Cloney, Joseph Holt and William Farrell). This initial splurge of misleading writing about the rebellion lasted until after Catholic Emancipation has been safely achieved.

By the 1840s, a second phase of writing began, which was much more explicit in acknowledging the revolutionary and republican principles of the United Irishmen, and their crucial role in organising the rebellion. This was explicit in the writings of RR Madden, Thomas Davis (the crucial populariser of Wolfe Tone) and Luke Cullen and reached its apogee in 1863, in the *Memoirs* of Miles Byrne, the last by an active participant in the events of 1798. Byrne's candid, forceful account of the United Irishmen in Wexford became a revered Fenian text - and also a problem for the institutional Catholic church. Given Byrne's highlighting of the leading role of Catholic priests in an oath-bound secret society, how did the church justify its strident anti-Fenian stance?

Father Patrick Kavanagh, a Wexford-born Franciscan, provided an elegant escape from this Fenian hook. Kavanagh developed a Catholic version of the rebellion as a crusade for faith and fatherland, devoid of United Irish influence. The rebellion itself was provoked not organised, its spread spontaneous, and its most important feature was clerical leadership - inevitably the heroic role of Father John Murphy. According to Kavanagh, the United Irishmen were irrelevant to the Wexford rising, thereby trumping the Miles Byrne/Fenian card; oath-bound secret societies were a liability, the only genuinely nationalist movement could be led by Catholic priests, who alone would provide selfless, dedicated leadership to the Irish people. Kavanagh's text is written explicitly against the backdrop of the lurid Cullenite assault on the Fenians and the obsessive clerical condemnation of secret societies. It is precisely for the same reason that Kavanagh overemphasises the dangers of informers and drink within secret societies.

Appearing originally in 1870, but rapidly going through multiple editions, Kavanagh's *Popular History* salvaged the rebellion for Catholic nationalists and dominated interpretation in the buildup to the centenary of 1898.

Kavanagh's sectarian version (he was vice-president of the Ancient Order of Hibernians, the Catholic equivalent of the Orange Order) quickly became hegemonic within this climate of opinion - and so dominant within Wexford, for example, that it may literally have repressed existing popular versions of the '98. It is this repression or clerical sanitising which accounts for the so-called 'silence' on '98 in the Wexford folk memory of the 20th century. After Kavanagh the 'mighty wave' of Father John Murphy swept all before it historiographically.

The 1898 Centenary

1798 occupied the place in the 19th century's imagination that 1641 had done in the 18th century. James Connolly could write in 1898:

> The mere fact that it is not yet possible to speak or write of '98 without arousing a host of storms, passions, hopes and fears proves undoubtedly that the cause which introduced such a host of apostles and martyrs in that fateful year is not yet a lost cause, and is not regarded as such either by friends or enemies.

157

The centenary followed on the very zenith of imperialism - the 1897 Jubilee Celebration for Queen Victoria's accession, which had been zealously marked in Belfast and Dublin. The nationalist riposte was to stage-manage 1898 as a rebuff to those who thought that Ireland might settle peaceably into an imperial niche. A Belfast Unionist, John Martin, writing in 1898, finished with this peroration:

The Union between Great Britain and Ireland must occupy a higher platform, as it is destined to achieve nobler issues, the progress and prosperity of a united people, whose name, prestige, and power among the nations are acknowledged; whose flag is honoured, whose trade is blest, and whose Queen and Empress was so recently honoured by the representatives of the nationalities of the world. The flag of England is fanned by the breezes of every clime; her commerce grasps the entire earth; the oceans separating continents are only her great highways; the "marriage ring" which binds them together in commercial activity, so that it may well be quoted, "The sea is England's glory, the bounding wave her throne." Let us not forget that august and princely tribute paid to our good Queen Victoria by the several nationalities of the world on the occasion of her Jubilee, the varied languages represented, the different nations and peoples all gathered to her hearth like children of a common family, not conquered by force of arms, but captivated by goodness, reform and progress. Had you witnessed that scene in London, you would have seen the natives of Hindustan, the savage tribes of North America, the Negroes of West Africa, the Maoris of New Zealand, Chinese, and Zulus and Kaffirs and tenants of the Oceanic Islands, vying with one another in honouring our own Victoria, side by side with the kings and princes of Europe, India, Japan and Siam, all joining with the many colonial representatives in bearing witness to England's goodness, to England's greatness and to England's model monarch. The only blot on the escutcheon of that memorable day was the apathy of the so-called Nationalists of Ireland. They apparently sulked, and could neither associate with savage nor civilised.

In June, the Grand Orange Lodge Master issued 'A Warning against the Proposed '98 Commemoration in Belfast':

..while we regard the proposed demonstration of June 6 as a flagitious display of sympathy with an armed insurrection which, above all things was characterised by a series of most foul and cowardly murders and

massacres of innocent men and women whose only offence was their
Protestantism, we fully recognise that it is for the constituted authorities
and for them only to say whether such demonstration is to be allowed
or prohibited. Loyal men and women are asked to attend with double
diligence to their business on 6 June and reserve themselves for the 12
July celebrations which are expected to be of unusual interest and
magnitude.

1798 still exercises the Northern liberal imagination, despite Edna
Longley's peremptory conclusion that in political terms "1798 is of no
more practical use than 1916". A more genuine engagement is evident,
for example, in the work of Stewart Parker, Tom Paulin, Brian Keenan
and Gary Mitchell. In a poem in his collection *Fivemiletown*, Paulin
reopens an imaginative space for the Presbyterian United Irishmen:

I traced them to the Linen Hall stacks -
Munro, Hope, Porter and McCracken;
like sweet yams buried deep, these rebel minds
endure posterity without a monument,
their names a covered sheugh, remnants,
some brackish signs.

Stewart Parker's play about Henry Joy McCracken, *Northern Star*,
looks at 1798 through the lens of the Northern 'Troubles':

Ancestral voices prophecy and bicker, and the ghosts of your own time
and birthplace wrestle and dance, in any play you choose to write - but
most obviously when it is an history play.

In a passage full of pathos and the sense of a missed opportunity,
Parker looks at the long-term consequences of the failure of 1798:

And yet what would this poor fool not give to be able to walk freely
again from Stranmillis down to Ann Street ... cut through Pottinger's
Entry and across the road for a drink in Peggy's .. to dander on down
Waring Street and examine the shipping along the river, and back on up
to our old house ... we can't love it for what it is, only for what it might
have been, if we'd got it right, if we'd made it whole. If. It's a ghost
town now and always will be full of angry and implacable ghosts.

Parker understood the import of the English radical William Morris's comment in 1887:

> Men fight and lose the battle and the thing that they fought for comes about in spite of their defeat and when it comes, turns out not to be what they meant, and other men have to fight for what they meant under another name.

Conclusion

The United Irish project of an inclusive, democratic, non-sectarian Ireland remains uncompleted. The 1798 rebellion remains buried under an oppressive weight of misrepresentation. By excavating its hidden meanings, 1798 can be made available in an entirely fresh way, opening an invigorating and generous space in which to consider it. 1798 cannot be claimed by any single political tradition in Ireland. The Catholic Nationalist version which dominated the centenary, 1938 and 1948 commemorations created the 1798 which people think they know. By getting behind these commemorations we reopen 1798 as an event in the history of Presbyterians as much as in the history of the Catholics. We restore the international perspective which informed the United Irish project, rather than seeing it as merely a set of cabbage-patch skirmishes.

We must also generously acknowledge the Ulster dimension to 1798, especially the enormous Presbyterian contribution, with its enlightened emphasis on justice, equality and civil liberty. In so doing, we restore a proud episode in their history which has been confiscated from them by a partisan historiography and their own complicity in convenient amnesia. We strive to liberate 1798 from the straitjacket in which historians have sought to confine it. The 1790s remain as a vision and an inspiration for the 1990s. As Walter Benjamin understood, to be forgotten is to die again:

> Only the historian will have the gift of fanning the spark in the past who is firmly convinced that even the dead will not be safe from the enemy if he wins and this enemy has not ceased to be victorious. ●

The Lost Writings,
James Connolly
Ed. Aindrias Ó Cathasaigh
Pluto Press
£13.99stg, 256pp

"What is the difference between the Unionist and the Home Ruler? Answer: Starting from the postulate that we accept Mitchel's definition of the British Empire, as 'a pirate institution robbing and plundering upon the public highway' we must conclude that the Unionists wish to keep the Irish people as *subjects* of the British Empire, the Home Ruler desires to raise them to the dignity of *accomplices*."

Thus wrote James Connolly in 1898, and such trenchant views are typical of the political journalism to be found in this book.

But, if we are able to call these writings journalism, because they were published in newspapers, this is a kind of journalism which can hardly be imagined in the current period, 100 years later. The series of papers in which Connolly wrote and often provided with a driving force, were intended to organise and to enlighten workers. They were not merely 'engaged' in social issues, they were intended to act as weapons in the class struggle, providing the information that the capitalist papers suppressed, expressing those demands which the workers were unable to themselves, offering ideas and connections for the trade unionist, nationalist and socialist activist to agitate on.

The areas which Connolly wrote about reflect the richness of his life, lived in Scotland, Ireland and the USA. He wrote for audiences in all three countries, but always as an internationalist and always as an Irish nationalist. Among the subjects he wrote about were: imperialism, especially that of Britain, but not hers alone; the link between revolutionary nationalism and revolutionary socialism; how to achieve a political representation for working people; exploring the dialectic between religion and socialism; exposing the appalling conditions in which

working people lived; making a constant critique of Irish middle-class liberalism; opposing the Partition of Ireland; railing against the carnage of the First World War and attacking its apologists.

But, as well as these better known areas of his thinking, which are written about in a style never less than passionately fluent, there can be found ideas of startling originality, dealing with human character and endeavour, which will surprise even the seasoned James Connolly reader. For instance, in an article on the 'spiritual inheritance of the Celt' he comments that: "You will hear a man or woman denouncing 'the gross materialism' of England as contrasted with Celtic spirituality one day, and the next you will find the same person showing a most laudable (?) but 'grossly material' desire to establish Irish manufactories where Irish wage slaves can be robbed by Irish capitalists; or joining with rackrenting landlords and scheming company promoters to demand an abatement of taxation on their own precious incomes." And this from a man who never heard of the Ansbacher Accounts!

Or, what about: "The influences which go to the destruction and debasement of the Irish Celtic character are not racial in their character, they are social and industrial; it is not Anglo-Saxonism but Capitalism which pours its cheap filth into our news-agencies, and deluges our homes with its gutter literature." Áine Ní Chonaill eat your heart out, there's no claiming Connolly as just an immigrant ... but then, wasn't he one, and an emigrant too? Connolly knew about racism, he wrote about one side of the picture as "the inflow upon our Irish shore, the record of the successive hosts of foreigners who came amongst us and, finding Ireland a green and pleasant land, chose to abide there and become bone of our bone and blood of our blood. But there is another side, viz, the going forth of the Irish ... Irish exiles served as soldiers in the armies of every sovereign in Europe for hundreds of years, lived and loved and

REVIEWS

married and left children speaking all the tongues of Europe."

It would easily be possible to make up the entirety of this review with quotations which demonstrate the originality and relevance of Connolly's thinking. His opposition to Partition is well known. He carried this opposition into the Irish TUC, when he addressed the delegate conference in 1914. He warned: "The Exclusion of Ulster, or any part of Ulster, is the fearful price we are asked to pay for our weakness as a nation - a price so dishonourable that rather than consent to submit such a question to the arbitrament of a vote all patriotic Irish men and women had better far consent to accept the destiny of being rebel slaves of England in an undivided Ireland, as preferable to contented accomplices of English statesmen in the partition of Ireland."

Connolly would no doubt, if he were alive today, have some very contrary opinions on events in the peace process, especially the posturing of the career politicians. He was very tactical in his proposals for action, but he never lost sight of the greater historical sweep. His was a generation which would look on with disbelief and contempt as people claiming to come from a Marxist tradition proclaim 'the end of history'.

For Connolly, there were truly things worth fighting for. On the 1st January 1916 he wrote: "... Ireland has seen herself betrayed ... The coming year may see her still linked to that enemy once more at peace with the world, and the 'Irish Nation' finally relegated to the mere status of a gallant tradition, as little useful politically as the Jacobite tradition is to Scotland." We may yet see Blairite Labour politicians in Scotland using the false decorative trappings of that very same Jacobite tradition in the service of the Union ...

This, in short, is a great book for those seeking to learn the traditions of radical social thought and action, though the main introduction, by Ó Cathasaigh, contains some personal statements, taking issue with previous publishers and editors of Connolly's works, perhaps with some cause, but definitely to no effect. In one extraordinary passage he says that 'lack of time' meant that the ruling East German Communist Party was unable to complete publication of Connolly's writings after 1987. 'Lack of time' brought about by the fall of the Berlin Wall!

Whether Connolly would have smiled upon the Partition of Germany and the Stasi staying in power a little longer, so that his works could have been published, is at least open to question. The inter-sectional introductions, however, are genuinely useful, as are many of the notes.

Connolly's day remains to come, but the thin thread of his ideas, which Pluto is helping stretch once again into the Irish and British working classes should be eagerly grasped 'by all the forces aspiring to social and political freedom.'

Harry Vince

Colonialism, Religion and Nationalism in Ireland
by Liam Kennedy
Institute of Irish Studies, QUB
£9.75stg 231pp

Sometimes the first question to answer on reading a book is: why has it been written? The title of Liam Kennedy's collection of essays gives little away and the essays themselves, taken from various places over a period of eight years, are non-sequential in any obvious historical or thematic sense. But a closer inspection reveals that Kennedy is utilising a kind of economic determinism in order to disprove various tenets of nationalist historical, cultural and above all else political, discourse as being romantic, notional and unscientific.

He ends the book in discussing what he calls the "MOPE (Most Oppressed People Ever) world view", which he labels "the seductive power of the Irish saga of oppression, misery and victimhood." This is a worldview he wants to challenge, by "re-envisioning" the past "independently of this paradigm". To achieve this end he has marshalled an obvious scholarship in order to challenge (deficient) nationalist views with (sufficient) 'neutral' and 'scientific' ones, which, on a closer inspection, can also be called pro-union, albeit with some distancing of the author from the more atavistic variants of that position, wherein, according to Kennedy, Ulster unionists match what he calls the blindness of nationalist leaders to the problem of ethnic diversity in Ireland "image for image".

In discussing the Irish Civil War and its effects he compares Ireland to civil conflicts in other countries, for example ex-Yugoslavia, America, Spain, the old Soviet Union, Turkey and the Armenians - in terms of the death toll per head of population, and concludes that, while a "residue of bitterness" remained, the Civil War was "both absolutely and relatively minor", with "the impact on the death rate for society in the Irish Free State being indistinguishable from normal years."

This is illustrative of the particularly loaded reductionism he employs, where statistics stand in for openly expressed opinion, although in this case the death rate in an ethno-political conflict is not strictly an economic statistic. He could, perhaps, perform the same trick in regard to the Troubles of the past 25 years in the North, making reference to the numbers killed in road accidents, and conclude that these have been relatively 'normal years.'

In reality, of course, the Treaty, the Civil War and the deep splits they engendered, left a mark on the political and economic system in the Free State, and then the Republic, which cannot be measured simply in terms of the number of dead. The whole system of politics has been formed by it, including the Labour Party, which could claim to have had no direct part. The Irish Civil War both expressed politics and created their organisation anew. Another look at von Clausewitz wouldn't go amiss.

Kennedy appears to have some trouble in imagining the flexible and contradictory interactions between economics and politics. For him economic statistics form the primary basis of scientific method, whereas politics seem to be a matter of being better able to tune in to objective economic trends, he wouldn't be too far from home if the PDs set up an all-Ireland version of the Adam Smith Institute. Discussing the economic thought of Parnell leads Kennedy to "hazard the generalization that a preoccupation - both intellectual and emotional - with the political, to the neglect of the economic, determinants of development is a characteristic failing of nationalist leaders in many countries in most time periods."

If only those Africans had known this and waited a few years, the place might not be so backward, eh? Kennedy's super-rationalism seems to have led him to the conclusion that nations would be better off under the foreign rule of 'more advanced' economies until their economies develop and they themselves can develop a set of 'original' and 'profound' ideas to go with independence.

This method of viewing problems - through what one might explain as a pseudo-scientific lens, also leads him to comment, about the process of emigration in the period after the Famine, that: "My own impression is that the outflow raised material living standards on average among those who remained at home and most certainly among those who emigrated to North America." Emigration was useful, according to the Kennedy method, because only "widespread industrialization could have generated jobs on the scale necessary to match the reproductive powers of the Irish family."

In another section he questions whether an independent Irish government, had one

REVIEWS

existed at the time, would have handled the Famine any better than the British,

Attempting to come at the politics of nationalism using tangential arguments, supposedly founded on 'hard' economic facts, he does not further the cause of objectivity. In trying to run a kind of 'on the one hand' and 'on the other hand' narrative, a sort of implied 'two traditions' argument in economic history, when he is discussing the economic effects of the Union, he slips in remarks like, "the economic interpretation of the Union became less rather than more sophisticated in the hands of militant Home Rulers and the ideologues of Sinn Féin." In front of such thinly cloaked prejudice one can only remark that a little less sophistication and a little more downhome intellectual rigour and honesty, not to mention a more open espousal of one's position, might be a good thing, even from an academic.

This is not an uninteresting book. It does contain facts, tables and references in abundance, but it feels too much like a book with a coy unionist agenda which has grown ever so slightly too big for the crypto-scientific bush it's trying to hide behind.

Harry Vince

The Women of 1798
Eds. Dáire Keogh
and Nicholas Furlong
Four Courts Press
207pp

This book opens with the words, "No aspect of the 1798 rebellion has been so neglected as that of the women's role in the events of that year." The purpose of the book is to start the work of remedying this omission.

But time and again the authors of the different contributions admit to being confounded by the absence of sources. Whether the chroniclers of the events of that year came from a republican or a loyalist perspective, they were united in either ignoring or not seeing the role of women, with a few exceptions.

The first person to attempt to write about these women was herself a woman, Helena Concannon, whose *Women of 'Ninety-Eight* was published in 1919. But, as the editors point out, those who inhabited her pantheon were all there by virtue of their relationship to their husbands, sons and brothers, and not in their own right, in line with the prevailing attitude to the place of women in the nationalist struggle.

This volume attempts to present the women who lived through, participated in and observed 1798 within the contexts of their own circumstances, but also as individuals in their own right. For some this is easier than others - for example, we know something of the lives of Matilda Tone and Mary Ann McCracken, even if these lives were previously appropriated to illustrate ideals of feminine republican virtue.

For someone like Bridget 'Croppy Biddy' Dolan, however, it is more difficult to disentangle myth from fact and draw even tentative conclusions about her motivation. She entered folk-history as a hate figure because of her role in giving evidence against numerous Wicklow United Irishmen in the court-martials which followed the suppression of the Rebellion. Her youth was spend consorting with boys and riding donkeys and, later, horses. She later acquired a reputation as a prostitute. To what extent was she destined to be a social outcast because of her youthful behaviour? Did this influence her rejection of friends and neighbours in her later betrayals? Or was it due to mere venality, as the evidence might suggest, with her acquiring clothing and money from the authorities in return for her evidence?

She shares with many of the women participants in the rebellion the fact that her low social status and its almost certain accompanying illiteracy means they could leave no record in their own words of their thoughts and deeds. Anna Kinsella points out that, "The women who fought in 1798 were, for the most part, low on the social scale and all to often their contribution is alluded to in the vaguest terms." She makes recourse to contemporary folk memory and ballads in an attempt to glimpse their participation, but the scale and details remain elusive. What is certain is that women were sworn to membership of the United Irishmen, and many fought in arms alongside men.

So inevitably most of this book concerns women who have left documentary trace, and therefore is a record of the involvement of women from higher up the social scale. With the exception of Bridget Dolan, all those examined in detail are Protestant, and include both those involved in the United Irishmen, albeit overshadowed by male relations, like Matilda Tone and Mary Ann McCracken, and those either passively sympathetic or on the other side.

There is no common theme, therefore, as the views and self-perceptions of the women featured in the book vary widely. So, indeed, do those of the authors. Some, like Eleanor Burgess, use the framework of 1798 to examine the lives and experiences of a particular woman, such as Edward Fitzgerald's aunt, Louise Conolly, while others, like Nancy Curtin, take the opportunity to examine the complex interaction between the emerging ideology of Irish republicanism and the creation of a space for women's political action (through the part played by Matilda Tone)

The book is tantalising in that it suggests a wider role for women in 1798 than it has been able to uncover. But it does provide a valuable start to work that can only grow.

Carol Coulter

Edmund Burke
by Conor Cruise O'Brien
New Island Books
£12.99pb 356pp

Conor Cruise O'Brien has a fascination with Edmund Burke which travels way beyond the simply historical. In some way he sees in Burke his own antecedent: heretic, principled loner, complex straddler of Ireland and Britain, campaigner against injustice in the colonies, polemicist.

Like Burke, Conor Cruise does not seem to see Ireland as exactly a colony. In this biography O'Brien interprets Burke as a force for Catholic emancipation, achievable by maintaining the link with Britain and not breaking it. O'Brien writes that "Burke, by contrast (to Wolfe Tone) and with some success, tried to utilize the connection with England for the benefit of all the Irish, Catholic and Protestant, as well as England."

O'Brien writes about the ambiguities in Burke's background: officially Protestant, but with a Catholic-tinged mother and other lurking shadows, like an apparent religious 'hiatus' in London.

He traces Burke's political and intellectual career with copious examples. For most of his life allied with the Rockingham Whigs, later to produce figures such as Charles James Fox, Burke opposed the taxation of the American colonies without extending them some kind of franchise. He tried to repeal the Tea Duty, without success and as the American War of Independence slipped inexorably into being he argued for conciliation. Burke called on the government and King George to "Let the colonies always keep the idea of their civil rights associated with your government ..."

A product of the period of the Enlightenment, in the sense of believing in rational argument as the source of policy, Burke nonetheless believed in social structures bordering on natural hierarchy. He said that "Men must have a certain fund

REVIEWS

of natural moderation to qualify them for freedom ..." This is the kind of idea that generations of liberal politicians have taken up with less eloquence since.

Burke was opposed to direct government by the masses. When the young Henry Grattan said that an MP was "the servant of his constituents, whose commands he was bound to obey", Burke rejected this. As the French Revolution unfolded some years later his view had hardened. He argued (and this provoked a breach with his friend Fox) that the National Assembly only had power "whilst they lead or follow the popular voice, in the subversion of all orders, distinctions, privileges, impositions, tythes, and rents ... but I very much question, whether they are in a condition to exercise any function of decided authority ..."

One senses, from this book, that O'Brien feels, like Burke, that today such forces of "chaos and darkness" are stalking the earth - how to keep the 'popular voice' from the 'subversion of all orders', that could be the thread linking biographer to subject.

Edmund Burke was not a reactionary. He disliked slavery and, after initially laying out the arguments for draconian behaviour by the East India Company he later protested the brutal and hypocritical exploitation of India.

A number of his reflections appear to be on the relationship between the need for personal and religious freedoms and the need for order, strong government and law.

Burke seems never to have seen the separation of Ireland from Britain as a means to either of these ends. He believed, probably as a result of his own personal experience if one follows O'Brien, that independence for Ireland would lead to Protestant domination in a different and perhaps worse local form. Quite where the 'moderating' influence of the English court and parliament could be found in inter-community affairs in Ireland O'Brien does not show. But Burke's position was that radical Whigs, like CJ Fox, who leaned in the direction of support for an independent

Ireland "did not understand that independence for Ireland meant for the majority not freedom but repression." Having been for American independence, in order the better to tie the colonies into Empire, Burke now took the opposite view on Ireland.

No doubt he was influenced by the arrival of more extreme political influences from France, but he never entertained the possibility of a freely entered into democratic alliance between Catholics and Protestants. His own conception was clear: "there is, and ever has been, a strong republican Protestant faction in Ireland, which has persecuted the Catholics as long as persecution would answer their purpose; and now the same faction would dupe them ..." into rebellion.

Is there a hint of anti-Protestant *animus* brought about by his own family's experience as *Marrano* (covert Catholic) Protestants?

O'Brien tends to dismiss the United Irish movement too easily, in the middle of his discourse on Burke, as, "The late rays of the Enlightenment, as they penetrated the mists of rural Ireland ..."

Oh, Conor, how little they knew, those bog-anarchists. If only they had understood, as Burke said, that they had "the balance of the empire, and perhaps its fate for ever in (their) hands." But perhaps they did know, and cared for a different future than partner in empire. How the 20th century came, in different ways, to express the pent up aspirations of the 18th!

Conor Cruise's biography of Burke should be read by all those who reduce the meaning of Irish identity to one place, one mythical blood line and one religion. It is not an antidote to those falsehoods, but it provides part of the proof that if a life is complex, dialectical and by definition incomplete then so is the art of biography.

Harry Vince

REVIEWS

Other books received

Revolution in Ireland
Popular Militancy 1917 to 1923
by Conor Kostick
Pluto Press
£12.00 pb 240pp

An in-depth study of working class action in the period which straddles the War of Independence and Civil War. Kostick takes a critical view of the relations between revolutionary nationalism and the working class, as well as instancing class conflict which took place interwoven with the national struggle. He also takes a critical look at the trade union and Labour leaders who succeeded Connolly. His view is generally that of revolutionary socialism.

Equality in Community:
Sexual Equality in the Writings of William Thompson and Anna Doyle Wheeler
by Dolores Dooley
Cork University Press
£14.95pb 460pp

A completely thorough working through of the lives and writings of two 19th century radicals. The book begins with twin biographies, with the aim of showing that Anna Doyle Wheeler was far more than mere associate to Thompson, who although far better known 100 years ago has himself suffered neglect. It continues with an analysis of Utilitarian philosophy, its relation to gender and to concepts like 'community'. Through close examination of texts it shows how these two thinkers influenced and formed each other.

Dolores Dooley also shows how Wheeler's "emotional negotiation" skills helped smooth relations between herself, Thompson and other radical thinkers of the time, without compromising the political integrity of those concerned. She points out that this is a particularly female skill, whose importance is often neglected.

Disaster and Development
by Neil Middleton and Phil O'Keefe
Pluto
£12.99 pb 190pp

This book is vital reading for the many thousands of people involved, as donors, collectors or volunteers, in Third World aid in Ireland. It is even more vital reading for politicians and policy makers.

There is very little that is "natural" about the economic and political disasters which cause famine and dislocation, according to Middleton and O'Keefe. Examining seven disasters they discern "the hands of the terrible triplets of Bretton Woods", and point out the role and interaction of political, social and economic forces, international and local, which bring them about. Of immediate relevance to political debate in Ireland is their criticism of the current official distinction between 'economic' and 'political' refugees. Economic refugees are forced to leave their countries by "the resource predators of the developed world and their local satraps." Although very few leave the immediate region, they are condemned as scroungers. They conclude, "There are solutions, there is a common sense which may prevail over the idiocies of capital ... but realistic expectation must remain grim."

Dancing to History's Tune
History, Myth and Politics in Ireland
by Brian Walker
Institute of Irish Studies, QUB
£8.50pb, 185pp

Seven essays designed to provide introductions to aspects of Irish identity, using symbols and events as cyphers. The essay on commemorations, for instance, gives an outline history of St Patrick's Day celebrations, the Easter Sunday festival and nationalism, the 12th of July and Remembrance Sunday. The general thrust is to try and place Irish particularities in an international, especially European, context.

167